T E DEMON
O MODERN

D1614428

THE DEMONS
OF MODERNITY

Ingmar Bergman and European Cinema

John Orr

berghahn
NEW YORK · OXFORD
www.berghahnbooks.com

Published in 2014 by
Berghahn Books
www.berghahnbooks.com

© 2014, 2016 John Orr
First paperback edition published in 2016

Library of Congress Cataloging-in-Publication Data

Orr, John.
  The demons of modernity: Ingmar Bergman and the European cinema / John
Orr.
      pages cm
  Includes bibliographical references and index.
  Includes filmography.
  ISBN 978-0-85745-978-7 (hardback) -- ISBN 978-1-78533-203-6 (paperback)
-- ISBN 978-0-85745-979-4 (ebook)
  1. Bergman, Ingmar, 1918-2007--Criticism and interpretation. 2. Motion
pictures--Europe--History--20th century. I. Title.
  PN1998.3.B47O88 2014
  791.4302'33092--dc23

                                                                  2013042951

British Library Cataloguing in Publication Data
A catalogue record for this book is available from the British Library

ISBN 978-0-85745-978-7 (hardback)
ISBN 978-1-78533-203-6 (paperback)
ISBN 978-0-85745-979-4 (ebook)

For Rosalind and Michael

Contents

List of Illustrations

Images appear in the print version only, before the Filmography.

Foreword

Maaret Koskinen

John Orr was 'old-fashioned' in the best sense of the word. That is, he was the kind of scholar you seldom meet anymore, simply because of the mere breadth of his interests – sociology, politics, literature, film, indeed culture at large. Yet it is precisely this kind of 'old-fashioned' scholarship that is needed for the future, not least because of its inbuilt desire to bridge both geographical and disciplinary boundaries.

As such John Orr's work is well known and needs no extensive reiteration here. But, given the subject of the present book, let us remind ourselves of Orr's previous publications on film at least from the last decade, before his untimely death in 2010. Here we find topics ranging from modernity and Dogme 95 to stardom in French cinema, and essays on directors such as Peter Greenaway, Derek Jarman, Terrence Malick, and Carl Theodor Dreyer. Here we also find a number of edited collections, most notably *Post-war Cinema and Modernity* (2000), *The Cinema of Andrzej Wajda* (2003) and *The Cinema of Roman Polanski* (2006). But first and foremost we find John Orr's own labours of love: *The Art and Politics of Film* (2000), *Hitchcock and Twentieth Century Cinema* (2005) and *Romantics and Modernists in British Cinema* (2010). The last book in this list should logically have been John Orr's final publication, had it not been for another labour of love – Ingmar Bergman, the Swedish director (1918–2007). It was this book about his films that Orr was in the midst of writing in the autumn of 2010, and which now, as fortune has it, can be published posthumously.

Since it was our mutual interest in Ingmar Bergman's work that brought us together, let me continue on a more personal note. John Orr and I met only once. It was on the occasion of the Ingmar Bergman Foundation's first international conference in Stockholm in 2005, which I, as representative of Stockholm University, had organized together with the other member institutions of the Foundation.[1] And to my delight John Orr agreed to write one of the extra chapters that we decided to commission for publication together with the conference proceedings, in a collection eventually entitled *Ingmar Bergman Revisited* (Orr 2008). The name of Orr's contribution was grand indeed, 'Bergman, Nietzsche and Hollywood', but certainly no disappointment. It was here that he began writing those parts in the present book that delve into Bergman films of the 1950s – Bergman's 'flair for translating the contemporary fable of classical Hollywood into European terms', as Orr put it in an early outline.

The next time we were in contact was by mail, when John Orr inquired about some detail regarding Bergman's film *The Silence* from 1963, about which I was in the midst of writing a book-length study at the time (Koskinen 2010). Not long thereafter Orr's fine essay appeared, called 'Camus and Carné Transformed: Bergman's *The Silence* versus Antonioni's *The Passenger*' (Orr 2007). Again, in this piece it is possible to detect the outline of those parts in this book that deal with the intricate and fascinating relations between Ingmar Bergman and his contemporary Michelangelo Antonioni – that 'intense preoccupation with the malaise of modern intimacy', which, according to Orr, these two filmmakers shared.

In short, what we find in *The Demons of Modernity: Ingmar Bergman and European Cinema* is precisely what the title promises, for this is the first book-length study of Bergman's films in a specifically European context – politically, philosophically and aesthetically. John Orr's contention is a seemingly simple one, namely, that Bergman, even in his heyday as art film auteur, was and still is regarded as a peripheral figure, culturally isolated from the rest of Europe. Thus the aim of his book is to dispel this as a myth in order to catch sight of Bergman again and reinstate him within a wider spectrum, indeed at the very centre of European film history.

Orr's book sets out to contextualize Bergman's work in a comparative fashion. It does so firstly by looking at Bergman's relationship to some individual European directors, from early Dreyer to contemporaries such as Michelangelo Antonioni and Andrei Tarkovsky (and, as Anne Orr notes in the afterword, the plan was to continue with more recent works by Michael Haneke and Lars von Trier). But the book also looks at Bergman's critical relationship to some key movements in film history. One is the French New Wave and the 'cinema of intimacy' – François Truffaut, Eric Rohmer and Jean-Luc Godard. In this context, Orr hones in on the reiterated notion that Bergman's modernism 'followed' Godard. But the truth is the opposite, Orr contends, and proceeds to illustrate to what extent Bergman's work in the early 1950s in fact served as a springboard for the modernism of the French New Wave. In this manner Orr unravels the intricate connections, not one-sidedly as film histories and historiographies generally would have it, but favouring instead the interplay and intertextuality of films that in his view made a vital contribution to European modernism in the 1960s.

John Orr had planned to look at Bergman and New German Cinema in the same vein, in a chapter entitled 'Bergman and the German Connection', from early Fritz Lang up to Margarethe von Trotta. In an outline of this unfinished chapter, Orr even calls Bergman's German-produced film *From the Life of the Marionettes* from 1979, 'a major (and unacknowledged) contribution to New German Cinema by a foreign director of a previous generation' – a surprising observation, yet perfectly head on.

John Orr manages, however, to step outside any narrow interpretation of the comparative framework, and does so through the notion of modernity, in all its complex and multifaceted aspects. Certainly, an important facet in the prism of modernity is the existential and philosophical oft-cited loss of faith – in religion, politics, and art; and that Bergman too gradually abandoned metaphysics in favour of the secular has certainly not gone unnoticed by previous scholars. But, as Orr wisely notes, in Bergman faith and its 'residues never quite evaporate: they linger in unsuspecting ways'. Very true; that lingering in fact can be said to encapsulate Bergman's entire *oeuvre*. Thus, in light of this lingering or residual effect, Orr contextualizes Bergman's development differently, detecting in his films strands of what he calls *demonic materialism* – a kind of residual demon embedded in modernity. This concept carries with it a number of advantages. Firstly it manages to nuance the (often) dualistic stances taken by previous scholars between the secular on one hand, and the metaphysical on the other. In Bergman, Orr contends, it is never a question of either/or, of unproblematic faith or purely materialistic secularity, but rather an ambivalent in-between-ness. His cinema, 'does not oppose the premise of demonic (as opposed to divine) intervention in human affairs', yet at the same time it is marked by that which Orr calls 'tragicomic yarns of human resistance to modernity'. This is an ambivalence, he contends, that separates Bergman from the metaphysical cinema of Dreyer and Tarkovsky as well as from the secular work of Godard and Antonioni, for all their similarities.

Secondly the concept of demonic materialism is informed in a fruitful way by recent film theory regarding the body, the embodied or haptic vision and role of the senses, in art as well as life.[2] Let me cite only one of many favourite passages from this book: 'Bergman's is a tactile cinema, a cinema of the flesh that rejects pure spirituality and brings the spectator up close and personal to the textures of the skin, of water, of sweat and tears ... Bergman's cinema is a celebration of the density of being, of the joys (and heartbreaks) of a material world.'

This 'carnal connection' in Orr's writing not only 'modernizes' Bergman for the purposes of academic study, clarifying to what extent his work is (still) a relevant object of research. More importantly it also opens up Bergman's films for more hard-core issues of the modern world, pointing towards a little researched area in the scholarship on Bergman, namely the sociopolitics of modernity. This line of inquiry is particularly relevant given the (in)famous Swedish model of modernity – the 'enlightened bourgeois domination and an effective welfare state', to cite Orr. In fact, it is all the more relevant now that this very same model has resurfaced more recently in Stieg Larsson's globally bestselling *Millennium* books, whose 'demonic' features have been splashed over screens transnationally (not least through David Fincher's remake of *The Girl with a Dragon Tattoo* in 2011) as certainly as Bergman's were fifty years ago.

Here John Orr hones in on certain aspects of the welfare state, all those medical doctors and psychiatrists (for instance in Bergman's *Face to Face* from 1976), and the idea of the caring professionals having been reduced to 'institutionalized compassion'. It is through such details and figures, according to Orr, that Bergman obliquely offers, 'a trenchant critique of a Swedish Welfare State based on precepts of rational social engineering', in which, 'the Enlightenment project as Swedish Social democracy seems a world away', concluding that Bergman 'sees its rational malaise as deeply rooted in the curse of modernity' (Hedling 2008).

In this way Orr's close readings open up far larger political issues at the core of modernity. It is particularly in the first chapter of this book that he hits a raw nerve – Bergman's adulatory brush with National Socialism during a visit to Germany as a teenager. Interestingly though, Bergman himself, with his characteristic showmanship, made sure to take charge of the issue, not least in his self-bashing autobiography, perhaps as a way to diffuse the issue. But to Orr this brush remains *the* demon that haunts Bergman's work – a prism through which it is possible to regard 'his strange, oblique relationship to living history'. It is this experience that made his cinema one of crisis, in which Bergman constantly 'wants to pinpoint the moment at which the 'rational' bourgeois subject ... defaults'.

In this respect Orr's analysis fruitfully dovetails with a book (which has been published in Swedish only) by David Aquilon. It too is one of those rare works that attempts to contextualize Bergman's films in a historical and political discourse, in this case by focusing on the recurring figures of text and body as cultural constants in Bergman's films, which in turn are incorporated in a discussion of the body politic at large. And although Aquilon's analysis revolves around Bergman's German productions, most notably *The Serpent's Egg* from 1977 (set in the Weimar Republic), his methodology is similar to Orr's. That is, while not shying away from the biographical and psychologically tinted readings of Bergman, both contribute to recontextualizing his films in the history of ideas and modern culture, setting up a dialogue with not only previous scholarship on Bergman but contemporary cultural and sociopolitical discourse as well (Aquilon et al. 2005).[3]

In focusing on modernity, Orr's book in effect also contributes to various transnational issues that have resurfaced on the agenda in film studies during the last decade (Durovicová and Newman 2010). If nothing else the concept of modernity (intrinsically transnational) helps clarify the inordinate degree to which Bergman has been regarded as a proponent and pillar of a (Swedish) national cinema, thus also becoming a playground for what Benedict Anderson famously called an 'imagined community' (Anderson 1991). In other words, Orr's approach helps to disperse geographical as well as imagined boundaries, including those residual and sometimes quite antiquated images of what is supposedly (nationally) Swedish, through certain intrinsically transnational phenomena such as genre and, indeed, modernity.

In a similar vein, Orr's approach also contributes in contextualizing and problematizing the notion of the auteur as a sort of free agent, as a curiously separate entity locked up in his own sphere of genius, seemingly freed from normal worldly constraints and various cultural discourses. Yet it is all wonderfully paradoxical. For there is no doubt that Orr is a staunch auteurist, one who revels in close reading, all the while creating trajectories across a filmmaker's works and several others as well. It goes without saying that this is risky business, since there is always a chance that such trajectories over temporal and geographical borders will result in comparisons that remain abstract and ungrounded. But although Orr performs his intertextual readings with decidedly auteurist underpinnings, the result is never abstract or set loose from larger contexts. He somehow manages to forge the details with the larger issues at hand, grounding his discussion of individual films in the ideologies, politics and dynamics of the floundering value system of a particular time.

Finally, let it be said that John Orr is simply a fine writer whose language is characterized by elegance and clarity. Indeed, at times his insights are chiselled out as veritable bon mots of Flaubertian flair. As just one example, let me cite his idea of anointing Bergman's major figures, 'psychic gladiators, only half-protected by the emblazoned shields of faith or reason'. Very nice; and why not – instead of that hackneyed, albeit iconic figure of the Knight battling with Death, as in Bergman's *The Seventh Seal* (1957)?

Ultimately, what stands forth in John Orr's last book is the legacy of an avid cineaste – all those experiences, thoughts and observations made during a lifetime of watching, teaching and writing on film that have sifted through layers of time and therefore have remained. As John Orr himself puts it, referring to how Ingmar Bergman's *Wild Strawberries* (1957) combines a double 'movement forward in space with the oneiric movement backward in time'.

At the same time there remain in this book oblique passages where you sense that the writer is on the verge of something more, and would have returned to it – but was cut short in his stride. These remain as kinds of symptomatic nodes in the text, all the more intriguing, and as if waiting to be unravelled. So be it: the ball has been set in motion so that anyone interested may pursue it further.

Notes

1. For more information on the beginnings of the Ingmar Bergman Foundation, see Koskinen (2010:16–18)
2. See for example, Marks (2000), Sobchack (2004) and Elsaesser and Hagener (2010).
3. This doctoral thesis was tragically cut short by the author's untimely death, and was therefore compiled by Aquilon's supervisors.

Bibliography

Anderson, B. 1991. *Imagined Communities: Reflections on the Origin and Spread of Nationalism*. New York: Verso.

Aquilon, D., L.G. Andersson and E. Hedling. 2005. *Magisk Cirkel*. Lund: Film International förlag.

Durovicová, N. and K.E. Newman (eds). 2010. *World Cinemas, Transnational Perspectives*. London: Routledge.

Elsaesser, T. and M. Hagener (eds). 2010. *Film Theory: An Introduction through the Senses*. New York: Routledge.

Hedling, E. 2008. 'The Welfare State Depicted: Post–Utopian Landscapes in Ingmar Bergman's Films', in M. Koskinen (ed.), *Ingmar Bergman Revisited. Performance, Cinema and the Arts*. London and New York: Wallflower Press, 2008, 180–93.

Koskinen, M. 2010. *Ingmar Bergman's* The Silence. *Pictures in the Typewriter, Writings on the Screen* (Nordic Cinema Series). Seattle: University of Washington Press.

Marks, L.U. 2000. *The Skin of Film: Intercultural Cinema, Embodiment, and the Senses*. Durham: Duke University Press.

Orr, J. 2007. 'Camus and Carné Transformed: Bergman's *The Silence* versus Antonioni's *The Passenger*', *Film International* 5(3), 54–62.

Orr, J. 2008. 'Bergman, Nietzsche and Hollywood', in M. Koskinen (ed.), *Ingmar Bergman Revisited. Performance, Cinema and the Arts*. London and New York: Wallflower Press, 2008, 143–60.

Sobchack, V. 2004. *Carnal Thoughts: Embodiment and Moving Image Culture*. Berkeley: University of California Press.

Filmography

Face to Face, (Ansitke mot ansikte). 1976. Ingmar Bergman.
From the Life of the Marionettes, (Ur marionetternas liv). 1980. Ingmar Bergman.
The Girl with a Dragon Tattoo. 2011. David Fincher.
The Serpent's Egg, (Ormens ägg). 1977. Ingmar Bergman.
The Seventh Seal, (Det sjunde inseglet). 1957. Ingmar Bergman.
The Silence, (Tystnaden). 1963. Ingmar Bergman.
Wild Strawberries, (Smultronstället). 1957. Ingmar Bergman.

CHAPTER ONE

Ingmar Bergman
The Demons of Modernity

The death of Ingmar Bergman at the age of 89 in 2007 marked the end of an artist who defined the twentieth century as much as Joyce, Picasso, Stravinsky, Eliot or Brecht, yet who was also an artist about whose talents many critics are still ambivalent. And an artist too whose story is like no other. For not only did Bergman grow up, like many artists of his generation, during a deep crisis in European Christianity; he also grew up under the shadow of European fascism. And unlike many who turned as a result to the far Left, he made a choice at an impressionable age to run to the far Right, to embrace the monstrous apotheosis of what George Orwell later called 'the boot in the face'. But he did so because he did not see it like that at all. What Bergman saw was the revolution of the new, idealism and salvation; not brutality and extermination. In later years his misjudgment came to haunt him and before we examine his founding role in the European film of the last century, we need to look at the context of these convulsions.

His memoir, *The Magic Lantern,* at times self-dramatizing, tells the story of his 1934 teenage stay in Southern Germany – an exchange visit to a Protestant clergy family living near Weimar. One day the family travelled to town where the sixteen year old saw for himself, at a mass rally addressed by Hitler, the enthusiasm that national socialism fired up in so many Germans. He presents himself as instantly sharing in that attraction, which entailed hero worship of the Leader (Bergman 1988:122–23). To the young reader of Nietzsche that he then was, this collective force would come to seem a new, exciting and delirious exoneration of the will to power. Back home this early admiration for the Nazi regime was shared by his stern clergyman father, Erik Bergman, and showed up even more strongly in the fanaticism of his older brother, Dag, who went on to promote the cause of national socialism in Swedish politics. National socialism was not only the Lost Cause of Bergman's early life, but, after the fall of Berlin in 1945, the Extinct Cause, the Wrong Cause, the cause that ended all causes and prompted him into consciously ditching politics for good. At times he paid for it. In the 1960s his young film student Roy Andersson, Marxist and committed, lamented Bergman's refusal to see politics as an integral part of cinema. In 1968 radical leftist students walked out of Bergman's lectures at the Swedish Film Institute on, of all people, Eisenstein. Obsessed by Vietnam in that same era, critics and partisans refused to see the deep political implications of his war film *Shame* (1968). The irony was that, despite Bergman's disclaimer and the verdict of his most vociferous critics, it was still possible to read politics into his films. Yet the readings would remain complex and oblique, the complete opposite, for example of Bo Widerberg's 1969 film *Ådalen 31*. Widerberg's film was a committed eulogy to the Swedish labour movement of the early 1930s and to its struggles, which finally resulted in the triumph of a Social Democratic Party that would remain in power in Sweden for over three decades.

For Bergman, the knock-on effect of catastrophic politics and its traumas spilt into that other arena of belief that went much deeper: a faith in God so fundamental to his strict Lutheran upbringing. If faith was more profound than politics, it also, crucially, failed to outlast it to any great degree. For the young Bergman, German national socialism seemed not to contradict the Lutheran piety instilled by his pastor-father and to offer it hope of a new form of transcendence – an aggressive movement outward into collective delirium that would resolve the inner torments of faith. In this strange portfolio, a pagan national socialism acclaimed by German Protestants seemed to have been the burst of renewal that his tormented faith needed so badly. As this dubious politics imploded in 1945 – it proved after all to be a politics of death and destruction – his faith seemed destined to follow in sorry aftermath. For after the war, a double dilemma had arisen that could scarcely be resolved by any Christian believer (of which there were millions) linked to the banner of the swastika. How could the Cause in which he had believed, help to create the absolute terror of the Holocaust? And how could his Lutheran God have allowed it to happen?

Bergman publicly voiced his anguish as late as the mid 1970s in interviews with Jörn Donner and on Swedish television, claiming that in learning about the camps after 1945 it was 'as if I had discovered that God and the Devil are two sides of the same coin' (Elsaesser 2008:176). Here, the lingering doubt around Bergman is the lingering one about those who lose faith because of the world's evil, in which they feel implicated. Ridden with guilt, does one lose faith in a God that exists, or does one lose faith in the existence of God? His 1963 film *The Silence* refers, in Bergman's words, to 'God's silence'. But it does not refer to God's nonexistence, or to Nietzsche's notorious 'death of God'. The issue, in a way, is never resolved. In Bergman the very act of filming seems increasingly at times to have been a tormented act of distancing himself from a diminished faith, in which, nonetheless, he remains entranced by occasional angels and tormented as ever by a multitude of demons. Yet, as he would be the first to admit, angels and demons in his visionary world were never too far from one another. In escaping from faith, then, he carried its torments with him. Its residues never quite evaporate: they linger in unsuspecting ways. As late as the 1970s, he had produced a detailed treatment at the request of Italian television for a *Life of Jesus*, to be shot in Bergman's scenario on his favoured Swedish location, the remote Baltic island of Fårö – much too austere and Nordic, one suspects, for his Mediterranean backers who then went elsewhere.

Bergman's third persona, beyond faith and politics, lay, of course, in that 'secular' alternative that absorbs the energies of both in the twentieth century – the innovations of modern art. In wartime, neutral (and hence unoccupied) Sweden he had left home after quarrelling with his father and become driven and bohemian, living frugally, writing plays and screenplays, starting to direct onstage and modelling himself on the famous predecessor to whom he owed so much: August Strindberg. When Bergman visited Paris in the postwar years and lived out briefly the attractions he found in Marcel Carné's 'poetic realism', his bohemian adventure had a self-conscious precedent. Strindberg had done his time in Paris as a bohemian artist, but also as one who went mad and thought himself the world's greatest scientist: an egocentric delusion that wafts through the pages of his Parisian memoir *Inferno*. Bergman may have had breakdowns in his workaholic life but he was never truly insane like his famous mentor. Yet he aspired to like greatness and he now means as much to world cinema as Strindberg had meant to world theatre by the end of his life. Bergman may not have gone mad but his cinematic visions of madness are at times controlled and terrifying statements of human extremity. From Strindberg he took much, and more so because he came to direct his mentor's work so triumphantly onstage in Stockholm, giving flesh and blood to those key motifs that link the two so tightly in their artwork: the fractious woe that is marriage, the aesthetics of chamber intimacy, and the bold expansions of the dream journey in Strindberg's later plays. Not only did he realize these motifs onstage in memorable productions for the Royal Dramatic Theatre, but he also transformed them into cinema, his cinema, where they became something quite different, extraordinary and unique.

Let us go back to Bergman's Weimar visit. It also produced, he recalls, a brief antidote to infatuation with Nazi rallies – a visit in town to friends of his aunt, a

Jewish family who played 'decadent' jazz and songs from the banned music of *The Threepenny Opera* on their gramophone. The Brecht/Weill lyrics moved the Swedish teenager in unexpected ways and he committed them to memory: the anti-Nazi family was, understandably, soon to emigrate (Bergman 1988:126–27). In the following years, the young devotee of Strindberg was loath perhaps to acknowledge the growing quandary this embryonic episode implies. The new politics he embraced with such enthusiasm had taken away from Germany the very liberties he still had in Sweden to pursue his love of innovation and modern art. In wartime he had a freedom to write for stage and screen not enjoyed by writers and directors elsewhere in Northern Europe. Norway, Finland and Denmark were, after all, occupied nations. As for Germany, a whole swathe of art forms had been decimated, including its newest form: the cinema. Billy Wilder whose *Sunset Boulevard* (1950) Bergman admired so much, and Fritz Lang to whom Bergman later paid homage in *The Serpent's Egg* (1977), had both headed west to freer climes. Hence Bergman was strangely privileged and contradictory, much like those British and French writers of the 1930s who applauded Stalin from afar during the period of the Great Purges, and were prone to the same double standards. Yet the Nazi occupation of Europe made things more poignant and also, in Sweden, much stranger. Europe's first true social democracy, which sided so strongly with the Republicans in the Spanish Civil War, became and remained neutral, probably with an eye to the fate of neighbouring Finland, which suffered the horror of a double invasion – first from the Soviets, which it repulsed, and then from the Nazis when it was brutally occupied. Thus Sweden, which might have been a sure-fire target, remained strangely excluded from Hitler's tyranny (though not from his political pressure); and in the absence of an occupying army, Bergman's career started to thrive.

Faith, politics, art – this was an exhausting agenda, and at times for Bergman a deadly triangle. Yet politics has been crucial for many great directors – Eisenstein, Welles, Godard and Fassbinder among them; faith has been embedded in the films of many others. One thinks immediately of Dreyer, Bresson, Hitchcock and Tarkovsky. Bergman was no different: and yet he was different. Those who embrace politics may alter over time but usually they have a continuous line of engagement. With him it cut his life in two. Those who engage faith so deeply never wholly reject it. Yet Bergman went very close. It is wrong to see the frightening God-spider of Karin's vision in *Through a Glass Darkly* (1961) as Bergman's personal nightmare fantasy, or as the opposite, the clinical sign of his final denial of a spent faith and its substitution by a self-conscious endorsement of profane art. He is, after all, exploring the terrors of a young woman's schizophrenic mind with all the aesthetic distance that entails. And here all pure idealism in politics or religion, you feel, has been gutted of its powers by Bergman's vision of a perfidious modernity. You sense that Bergman is filming the effects of volcanic eruption after the event, exploring in close detail the cratered earth, the void left behind, the void in which human compassion smoulders like the embers of a dying fire; and all the while demons continue to haunt him. Love in spite of hate, care in spite of cruelty. Is this modernity then, the afterlife of the demonic after God has vanished? Are these the final residues of modernity still haunted by evil? Are they stacked up as the barest props on an empty stage? Or do they too disappear in a world of isolation and invisible terror?

There is a balance of sorts to all this. Now and again Bergman finds a riposte and a welcome refuge in laughter. After the dark and drab postwar years, he applies the fast pace of Hollywood comedy to 1950s Sweden in *Waiting Women* (1952) and *A Lesson in Love* (1954) where the sensibility is close to that of the great German émigrés Ernst Lubitsch and Billy Wilder. Later he goes back to the decade just preceding his own birth – one thinks of the delicate memory-scenes in *Wild Strawberries* (1957), or the sprawling tableaux of *Fanny and Alexander* (1982) that incorporated elements of his own childhood. Here the figure of the young Alexander reminds us of that childish immunity to the deadly triangle of Bergman's adult life and its agonizing choices. Immune to the weary cares of art, faith and politics, Alexander can retreat into a world of pure magic, of coloured slides and puppet shows, goblins and fairies that exist in the shadow play of the everyday world and precede the magic world of the moving image. It is a kind of innocence trembling on the verge of experience, but still serenely immune. For Bergman there is always a fallback position too, beyond the failure of hope in the art of performing, so that his motley entertainment troupes in *Sawdust and Tinsel* (1953) and *The Face* (1958) can elicit a fair share of our ribald laughter and echo our sense of hope in human buoyancy and invention. Through laughter too, Bergman often sought affirmation of life in a past age. As a consequence his turn-of-century *Smiles of a Summer Night* (1955), which so influenced Woody Allen, remains one of his most uplifting comedies because it works as an observed period piece where life and laughter finally triumph over doubt and darkness. Even in his two most sombre decades, the 1960s and the 1970s, there are flashes of farce, with mixed results. In 1960 the Don Juan parody of *The Devil's Eye* would precede the darkness of *Through a Glass Darkly* and, in 1964, the forbidding bleakness of *The Silence* (1963) is followed by the whimsical *All these Women*, for many critics a piece of fluff despite its comic touches and sharp self-mockery. And in 1975, after the intense, sombre intimacies of *Cries and Whispers* (1972) and *Scenes from a Marriage* (1973), Bergman filmed his flowing and lyrical tribute to Mozart's *The Magic Flute* which many rate as one of his finest achievements.

By the end of the 1950s, the tone and direction of his filming had, however, changed. From *Through a Glass Darkly* right through to *Autumn Sonata* (1978), it is mainly the contemporary world – bourgeois and prosperous but full of risk and sorrow and steeped in the climate of the Cold War – that brings forth the most tragic and disturbing of his films. Here Bergman's political nightmare does not really go away but abruptly changes course, and during these two decades pervades his cinematic vision. The Cold War had become a form of cool apocalypse, a menacing and ever-present backdrop, while Swedish social democracy seemed the epitome of a concerned, caring society whose professionalism could not finally deliver happiness, even among its own professionals. Here the purveyors of care are of course as much the victims of sorrow and desolation in Bergman's cinema as their disturbed clients. One thinks of Jenny Isaakson (Liv Ullmann) the psychiatrist suffering total breakdown in the claustrophobic *Face to Face* (1976). But his professionals can also be sinister and malevolent: discursive Dr Caligaris in a post-expressionist world. And while Bergman's bourgeois characters of this period may be rational autonomous beings, now surrounded by the good things of life, they are still strangled by the conflict between their polyvalent needs and the imprecise obligations of their faltering intimacies. And strangled means asphyxiated. Metaphorically speaking, all breath seems to expel itself from their bodies. It is not only marriage that can suffocate – Bergman's legacy from Strindberg – in these films it is intimacy as such, where in any relationship each troubled subject can in turn be perpetrator and victim, tormentor and tormented. At times, in *Cries and Whispers* and *Autumn Sonata*, this becomes a living hell. Here Swedish social democracy as an Enlightenment project seems a world away, refracted at best as a mixed blessing. At best the mockery is tongue in cheek. At worst it seems that Bergman sees its rational malaise as deeply rooted in the curse of modernity. For modernity's varied rationales and technologies are real, irresistible temptations: they give you open access to knowledge and material progress, which, in spite of everything, you really do want. But from this the question of human happiness is abruptly severed and promptly subtracted. Bergman stands on the threshold of the new consumer age, which is destructive of all value. Prophetically he saw it as a wager in which few gain and most stand to lose.

The other feature of Bergman's ambivalence towards the modern is the life of the city. In the films after 1955 the Swedish city is largely conspicuous by its absence. Not consciously so, but there is a gradual leaving, a departure and a not coming back. During his early films, the city – Malmö, Gothenburg, Stockholm – was a constant factor in his narratives: detailed and heavily stylized by studio interiors, at worst a Nordic pastiche of Carné's poetic realism, the French idiom that became one of Bergman's early loves in the cinema. In his hands, sadly, the poetry often evaporated. Working with tight budgets, mise en scène could be drab, dreary and leaden. There were scintillating exceptions – the Paris in the middle episode of *Waiting Women* or the Gothenburg of *Dreams* (1955). But often his city exteriors seemed functional, unadventurous, a tendency echoed many years later in his Stockholm-based television film shot on 16 mm, *Scenes from a Marriage*. In Bergman there is nothing resembling the southern architectural visions of Fellini or Antonioni, or the natural city curiosity that powered the French New Wave through their inspired explorations of 1960s Paris. For all the time Bergman spent in it as a stage director, Stockholm is nowhere much in his cinema as a living presence. He himself complained that it was unnaturally placed in the country, too northern, too bleak, and like an elaborate extended village surrounded by water and by forests.

With the early films, the spectator almost craves for a topographical escape, and early on this was something that Bergman increasingly found in Stockholm's summer archipelago. Brief sequences in *To Joy* (1950) and *Three Strange Loves* (1949) escalate into long triumphant passages among the islands in *Summer Interlude* (1951) and *Summer with Monika* (1953). Both films, the latter with its impulsive performance from Harriet Andersson, then became, as we shall see, the model for adventure and free spirit among the French New Wave. At one level Bergman created virtue (or art) out of necessity. Stage directing for three seasons allowed him the fourth, summer, for shooting feature films. And where is better than on the islands, to make use of natural light, of northern light, of midsummer light? Even though, as he insisted, Nordic summer light could have the quality of nightmare, and, for Isak Borg's celebrated coffin-dream in *Wild Strawberries*, most certainly does. Yet *Summer Interlude*, released in 1951, remains Bergman's purest and most romantic archipelago film. It starts with the recovery by Marie, a thirty-year-old ballerina, of a notebook belonging to her first lover Henrik during her distant teenage years. Koskinen has noted that the Henrik notebook that triggers Marie's memories of her island romance had a reflexive source in Bergman's rediscovery of a missing notebook containing the fictionalized story of his teenage love affair before the war (with a girl who then contracted polio) on which his island screenplay, co-written by Herbert Grevenius, is roughly based (Koskinen 2002:23). The film had been planned during Bergman's early postwar years as a flashback film about the pre-war period, but took several years to reach fruition. When it came, it was a triumphant breakthrough out of his postwar blues, a film about an idyllic pre-war age that was now over; a film that would briefly reinstate enchantment over disenchantment, love over cynicism and innocence over experience, without ever toppling the balance between them. For the film contains both, though succinctly unstated: the age of innocence before September 1939 and the age of experience after May 1945. Translated into the chronology of Bergman's career, they form the brief moment of romanticism, followed by the long period of modernism.

In the new chamber intimacies of his modernist period from 1960 onwards, the island setting continues as the archipelago is replaced by Fårö and the Swedish city is eliminated almost entirely. That is why his great American admirer, Woody Allen, is so unlike the Swede. Much of Allen's work is set in that one central borough of New York City: Manhattan. Where Allen lived, he filmed. The same had been true for Bergman, but with a difference. In 1960 with *Through a Glass Darkly* he came to film where he later built his home, on the remote Baltic island of Fårö, a militarized farming island north-west of Gotland; and in Stockholm hardly at all. Indeed, when he chose to make his most conventional, bourgeois and Americanized feature, *The Touch* with Elliot Gould in 1971, he set it in the town of Visby on Gotland, not on the mainland. When he returned to Stockholm as a location, it was in *Scenes from a Marriage* – a television film that was mainly interior and where residential areas of the city are shot without inspiration. Yet in a way it detracts not. For often Bergman abstracts and isolates his characters from their urban habitat, or entraps them so much within its interior spaces that we begin to question, through their lives, the nature of modernity itself. These are bourgeois lives in comfortable homes, yet bereft of cityscape, surrounded instead by landscape and seascape that is often barren and pitiless. There are no suburbs either. As such, 'transplanted', his subjects appear vulnerable and exposed.

Transplanting Equals Abstracting: Bergman's Transition to Modernism

The transplanted ensemble, the micro-group, the dyad or triad often linked by family and marriage, are freed from the detail of normal surroundings. One thinks of the island summer home in *Through a Glass Darkly*, the hotel in the foreign city, Timoka, that is the pivotal place and space of *The Silence*, the remote island retreat in *Persona* (1966), the country house in *Cries and Whispers*. The vision is freed up and abstracted: it creates its own cinematic space, its own world. Here the physiognomy of the face becomes vital, not only as the emotional centre of the body, but also of the filmic world itself. Bergman captured the look of the emotions more than any other European filmmaker, except perhaps for Dreyer. Here film and dream intermingle, sometimes as daydream, sometimes as nightmare. Narrative becomes oblique and plot is unresolved. Ambiguity is everywhere, in every word, in every gesture, in every cut. The mise en scène follows suit. There is no rural idyll here in Bergman's settings. The island retreat and the rugged coastline are recurring tropes of threat and fear. This is a barren isolated world so that the great loneliness Bergman detects in the Swedish psyche is played out on Swedish landscapes at their most forbidding, where they are objective correlatives, visual forms, of the desolate modern soul. For the modernist period, Bergman's vision remains primarily in black and white, and when in colour, the colour is drained out, desaturated, as in *A Passion* (1969), or richly concentrated – the deep blood-red textures that intersperse so precisely the rich black and white hues of *Cries and Whispers*.

The middle-class Swedes of two very different periods, the decade before Bergman's birth and the two decades of his mature adult life, are thus more open to examination. In the latter instance, Leif Zern and Erik Hedling have both seen Bergman's work as a trenchant critique of a Swedish Welfare State based on precepts of rational social engineering (Hedling 2008:180–93). Freed from city and suburb, the bourgeois family, or its dismal remnants, are opened up to microscopic study. In modern times the failing marriage is cruelly deconstructed: the minefield of sibling relations explodes at periodic intervals. For films of the present day, the flaky underlay of social democracy in its prime is magnified, to our supreme curiosity and discomfort. And Bergman is nothing if not ingenious. Instead of shipping his civilized bourgeois to a faraway desert island to strip away their cultural veneer, he ferries them, in the case of Fårö, to a Baltic island only just within territorial waters. This is far more fascinating: his troubled subjects are half inside their culture of civility but half outside it as well. In and out, a deadly formula, and one that has been devoured by devoted cinephiles throughout the second half of the last century. In truth Bergman's subjects are never fully barbarians nor are they fully rational beings. They oscillate between one end of the spectrum and the other, unable to abandon the primitive for the cultivated or the cultivated for the primitive. That, above all, is what defines his crucial work of the 1960s and 1970s. Social progress is no rational blueprint for the highly educated to follow to its civilized endpoint. It is a short-term loan with escalating interest rates and Bergman wants to pinpoint the moment at which the 'rational' bourgeois subject (always an ideal, never a reality) defaults. And in his best work he captures that instant for posterity.

Nightmare's After-Effects

In the postwar period Bergman may have renounced politics, but its after-effects linger throughout his long career. One vital point is clear. Rejection of fascism did not entail rejection of Germany. Historically, Germany had nourished a vast culture in art, theatre, music, writing and film that Bergman greatly admired; a culture that had long preceded the catastrophe of Nazism, but also survived and outlasted it. Bergman's love of Bach is well known, the influence of E.T.A. Hoffman and the German Romantics powerfully intermittent. And from his point of view German Expressionism, which he had absorbed into his cinema and his theatre, had in turn absorbed the legacy of his beloved Strindberg. When faced with the unexpected dilemmas of tax exile in the 1970s, it was to Munich, not Paris, that Bergman temporarily migrated. Yet another fundamental issue is anything but clear: the way in which Bergman's cinema functions as an exorcism of personal trauma and guilt. Here his dawning recognition after 1945 of the true extent of the Holocaust would have been a defining moment for him. Yet if trauma's aftermath affected him, it existed mostly in his work, not in his life. We could even say that perhaps it did not damage his life because it percolated through his art. Adorno had suggested that after Auschwitz there could be no poetry, but Bergman was raptly intent on creating a poetic vision of the world. Postwar paralysis did not afflict his work. If anything, trauma's aftermath made him even more driven: his energies never flagged. Yet the darkness of much of his cinema cannot be disentangled from his strange, oblique relationship to living history. And you sense here some kind of opaque transfer, an art sublimation that dare not speak its name.

For sure, his tangled encounter with Germany echoes faintly but discernibly through his films down the years. In his first realized screenplay *Torment*, directed in 1944 by Alf Sjöberg, Sjöberg turned Caligula – the cruel Latin teacher in Bergman's script – into a crypto-Nazi. In his postwar melodrama *Three Strange Loves*, heavily shadowed by Marcel Carné, his moody introspective 'hero' makes a train journey from Berne in Switzerland back through a ruined Germany to his native Sweden. One of the abiding images is that of starving platform hordes begging food from passengers at train windows as the express pulls into a German station. It remains for its time, one of Bergman's few explicit references to the war, and it is Germans who are suffering. Later, in *The Silence*, Bergman's intent was to create the nightmare of a foreign city where everything remains inscrutable and sinister. For this he drew in part on his brief visit to Berlin at the end of his student exchange in Weimar two decades previously. In *Persona*, actress Elisabet Vogler (Liv Ullmann), sees a famous war photograph and identifies the fate of a Jewish boy being rounded up for deportation by SS Guards in Krakow with that of her own neglected child. Finally in *The Serpent's Egg*, set in a 1923 crisis-ridden Berlin and shot in a Munich studio, he pays homage to Weimar cinema, to the street films of Lang, Pabst and Joe May made at Babelsberg, and, atmospherically, to the tight paranoia of Lang's Mabuse films; but with an added currency, with rampaging fascist paramilitaries and the retro-knowledge of political disasters to come. The sullen post-1945 rebel earlier played by Birger Malmsten, a figure isolated and existential, is replaced here by a different kind of earlier post-1918 maverick, a Jewish acrobat from Riga played by David Carradine, already alert to the anti-Semitic impulses on the streets of a dismal, destitute Berlin. The politics of despair all around him gives to Carradine's Max Rosenberg (Bergman's first and only Jewish rebel) a nervier, more desperate edge than any of the roles given to Malmsten, and his nomadic desperation in a starving Berlin is a portent of things to come.

In his only war film *Shame* however, Bergman had reserved his greatest piece of virtual history for Sweden itself, in his domicile island of Fårö, geographically speaking one of the country's most exposed outposts in the Baltic. What if the Nazis had invaded Sweden as they had Poland, tearing up yet more pieces of paper that 'guaranteed' neutrality? Or what if the Soviets had invaded Sweden as they had Finland? In either virtual scenario, who would have resisted? Who would have betrayed, or been betrayed? Where is the thin line drawn between partisan and quisling? And how quickly do the respectable bourgeois become refugees, the

lineaments of their assured social life ripped to pieces? How quickly do the things
. we all take for granted fall apart? You feel Bergman here is on much surer territory
in which he cleverly matches local detail to visual abstraction, sketching out a
modernist history that is the very opposite of the costume drama, an ingenious
and visceral virtual history that is past, present and future all in one. And you also
feel the final apocalyptic film of Tarkovsky, *The Sacrifice* (1986), about which
Bergman had mixed feelings, would have been impossible without his own, shot
as it was on the neighbouring island of Gotland with Bergman's loyal
cinematographer Sven Nykvist, who had begun work for the Swedish master in
Sawdust and Tinsel over thirty years previously.

One of the key secular features of Bergman's contemporary cinema is the role
of the caring professional: the academic or the doctor or the psychiatrist, whose
actions seem to embody the local expression of a caring society for which Sweden,
as a long-standing social democracy, has a powerful reputation, but which was
also a feature of Western Europe generally in the second half of the twentieth
century. Yet in Bergman the caring professional operates on the shifting sands of
institutionalized compassion. While Bergman often has an unerring gift for
revealing compassion at the heart of cruelty, he equally has a gift for insinuating
indifference or cruelty at the heart of compassion. This motif recurs throughout
many of his later pictures but is at its most subtle and strong in *Through a Glass
Darkly* and the Munich-produced *From the Life of the Marionettes* (1980). Just as
the doctor–patient relationship encourages care, it also encourages confession:
the flipside that Bergman often hones in on as the confession phenomenon. This
seems odd coming out of a tight Lutheran culture and not an obvious continuation,
rather in Bergman something post-religious – the power to speak out openly
about the intimate nature of one's life.

In Bergman, long before the present cult of media confession where,
electronically speaking, more or less anybody can be invited to discourse publicly
on anything deemed in a previous era to be strictly 'personal', Bergman connects
confession to intimacy but also to power. The elements of care and confession
that are part of his culture, and his films, are tied in to the general power struggles
and role reversals he associates with intimate life, between lovers, between
spouses, between siblings, between parents and children. Thus the ideology of
care that dominates European democratic societies is undercut by the micro
power struggles that form part of intimacy, that agonistic field of the human that
Bergman cultivates assiduously as his films withdraw from the arena of public life.

Let us finally turn to aspects of family life as Bergman sees them. In his period of tax exile in the 1970s he made *Autumn Sonata* in Norway with Ingrid Bergman and Liv Ullmann. Generally dismissed as late in the cycle of chamber drama and often repeating the tropes of his previous films, it remains one of his most powerful works. In it the chamber drama becomes a psychic chamber of horrors, a legacy no doubt of Ibsen and Strindberg, but one that Bergman fashions in his own way. Even when nothing spectacular happens, the pain is manifest. People cannot escape their kinship or their past, which often comes back to haunt them. Both *Autumn Sonata* and Bergman's last film *Saraband* (2003) begin with visits that are returns to a previous relationship that has fashioned a life – and still continues to do so. *Autumn Sonata,* so late in the *Kammerspiel* cycle, brings it to fruition precisely because it does not involve madness or suicide or death. *Saraband* is a television sequel to Bergman's popular serial television drama of the 1970s *Scenes from a Marriage,* involving as it does, the chance reunion of Marianne (Liv Ullmann) and Johan (Erland Josephson) in old age. But here Bergman goes beyond the vanities of marital strife and betrayal that mark out his superior television soap, deep into the long-term horrors of family life itself – seen now as something diseased and rotten to the core – even when its perpetrator–victims act with the best intentions. But the revelations are really in the conclusions that viewers have to draw for themselves. Bergman points the way, but completion, as in all his great films, comes through the eyes and ears of the spectator.

The Post–Nietzschean Wager 1: The Community of Film

Bergman's concept of filmmaking, as of his stage work, was collective. It worked both against the individualized bohemianism of his wartime life and against its absolute opposite, the disciplined hierarchies of national socialism in his pre-war life, which continued to linger residually until after the fall of Hitler's Germany (Bergman 1988:7–8). In a way it resolved that paradox: on the one hand the lone rebellious spirit, and on the other the fanatical search for a new kind of collective salvation on this earth that had collapsed in ruins. Yet even here Bergman, like nearly all aspiring artists, was a mass of contradictions. The defiant loner got married for the first time (but not the last) in 1943 and soon started having children. His second marriage followed in 1945. In the postwar years, the egotistic director, who preened himself in a leather jacket and tilted black beret for his film shoots while sporting a goatee beard, was also mired in a family life that drove him to distraction. Of his second marriage to Ellen Lundström, with whom he had four children and lived in a crowded Gothenburg apartment – along with the sick daughter from his first marriage, plus his new mother-in-law and her small son – he later wrote dramatically: 'Home seethed with crying children, damp washing, weeping women and raging scenes of jealousy, often perfectly justified. All escape routes were closed and betrayal became obligatory' (Bergman 1988:154). In fact, betrayal was not obligatory and the escape routes were open. Bergman, cunning to the end, always publicly prevaricated, veiling the circumstances of his own life, while appearing to make intimate confessions about them. Commuting to Stockholm to work in the theatre, and to the archipelago in the summer for film shoots, actually gave him plenty of creative opportunities. But his subjective sense of personal enclosure, of no exit, clearly found its way into the look and feel of his postwar films and often deadened them. In the years of austerity, Bergman, the serial seducer, was nothing like Camus and Sartre, his existential idols and serial seducers themselves amid the elegance of Saint-Germain-des-Prés. He was all but destitute, making maintenance payments and deeply into serial remarriage, investing statistically and emotionally in an institution that his life undermined until his final marriage in 1971 to Ingrid von Rosen, which lasted until her death in 1995.

His politics – or lack of it – was just as contradictory. A Jewish student called Erland Josephson was to become a lifelong friend and acted in many of Bergman's great films. In 1943, Bergman, the ex-teenage admirer of Hitler, helped produce an allegorical anti-Nazi play, *Niels Ebbesen* by Danish writer and cleric Kaj Munk, soon to be killed by Nazi collaborators in Denmark. On the occasion of Munk's death, Bergman duly paid joint tribute to the Dane with Victor Sjöström (Cowie 1992:26–27). Acting in that production was Anders Ek, soon to portray Camus's *Caligula*, not as an existential hero but as a demented Hitlerian madman, in Bergman's 1946 Gothenburg production of the new French play. Caligula was also the nickname of the tyrant Latin teacher in Bergman's debut screenplay of 1944, *Torment*, directed by Alf Sjöberg, who embellished this authority figure with pointed pro-Nazi details, including a visual resemblance to Himmler. In a way, Bergman is exorcizing his political demons, or trying to. In postwar Gothenburg, he had to bind together a theatre company still divided by pro- and anti-Nazi sentiments (ibid.:53) and his memoir contains the occasional ambivalence. Recalling late on in 1944, when the sound of American aircraft out at sea had drowned his Macbeth rehearsals in Helsingborg, he refers to the 'increasingly black headlines' in the newspapers

(Bergman 1988:146). But 'black' for whom? Then he notes soon after the war that a great veteran of the Swedish stage, whose career was at an end, was all too happy to blame his fate on the upstart director whom he called 'Hitler-Bergman' (ibid.:186). And talking of the trademark beret and goatee beard of the late 1940s, we might note the Nazi pastor-father of the blond Hannes, his pre-war German exchange pal, is described as, 'a slight man with a goatee beard ... and a black beret pulled low down over his forehead' (ibid.:119). A postwar double coding for the director perhaps – existential bohemian and demonic militant? Passing observations, but also revealing ones. The past was never quite over.

In 1960 James Baldwin, sounding opinions before a Bergman interview for *Esquire*, notes that in the early days many who worked for him found his attitude inflexible, his aggression – throwing hard objects at actors, through glass or against walls – impossible, and called him 'the demon director'. Baldwin's own encounter with the Swede prompted a slightly different claim. There was something in his 'weird, mad Northern Protestantism that reminded me of the black preachers of my childhood' (Baldwin 2007:18). The fanatical strain was still there, but by this time something had changed. Bergman had become a movie success and he had recruited, over the years, a team of cast and crew who became as loyal to him as he to them. Gone was the pseudo-dictatorship based on insecurity, to be replaced by an authoritarian leadership based on talent and observation. There was a shrewd attentiveness to the potential of all his cast and crew, a recognition not only of their worth, but a recognition that his worth depended on their worth. Bergman cunningly combined it with his esoteric will to power. And throughout the hothouse atmosphere of the stage rehearsal or the film shoot, Bergman was sharp enough to observe human behaviour in all its vanity, its aspirations, its foibles and its weaknesses – and to seduce beautiful actresses. By 1952 he was directing at the municipal theatre in Malmö, after stints in Helsingborg and Gothenberg, averaging two to three productions a year. From his various theatre companies and other stage venues, he would cast the film actors whose work repeated itself so triumphantly down the years: Gunnar Björnstrand and Anders Ek, his pre–Malmö actors, were joined by Harriet Andersson and Bibi Andersson, Max von Sydow, Ingrid Thulin, Gunnel Lindblom and many others. It was the makings of a tight film community, the start of a long collaboration with Gunnar Fischer and later Sven Nykvist as his cinematographers, with Nils Svenwall and later P.A. Lundgren as his art directors, and with Erik Nordgren as his musical composer.

Bergman was still a strong, demanding figure – at times autocratic. But the film community, like the theatre community, was the perfect antidote to the Nietzschean fantasies of the artistic loner. There was no point in trying to be an *Übermensch*: fulfilment lay in the relationship with others and thus making Nietzsche work in alternative ways. As a filmmaker Bergman is an actor's director, and in that respect at the very apex, I would argue, of European cinema. Yet, like many artists, he would neglect or abandon that other key dimension running through his life, the spouses, lovers and children he had left in his wake. Many social commentators of the mid twentieth century had naively argued that in modernity the nuclear family and the warm security of home and hearth were a refuge (for men of course) from the travails of a professional life, and created a perfect foil to a daily ethos of tough competition. With Bergman, it seemed the exact opposite. Fiercely competitive, the film community was often a refuge from the demands of the families he himself had created. At the same time his guilt and rage over his perfidies translated perfectly into the substance of his films. Increasingly, they came to illuminate the intimate dynamics of neglect and abandonment in our culture and did so in subtle, intricate ways that no other filmmaker was able to. It became a constant yet supple and variable theme from *Through a Glass Darkly, The Silence* and *Persona*, right up to *A Passion, Autumn Sonata* and *From the Life of the Marionettes*. And it was to be shattering.

To balance the art of chamber intimacy his film work is also reflexive, and the performing troupe, or if you like, travelling players, become a key element as a collective subject in many of the films. For Bergman cinema had its own theatricality. Yet he found no cosiness in the idea of the performing group. There is no utopian community to be found. The professional humiliations of his early days resonate through *Sawdust and Tinsel*. In *The Face, The Silence* and *The Rite* (1969) the travelling players all have a disturbing otherness, while in *Persona* performance itself become tragically monstrous. For sure, there is passing celebration of performance as magic and uplifting in *The Seventh Seal* (1957) and *Through a Glass Darkly*. But these are brief moments of enchantment in very sombre films and Bergman's performers are out on a limb: a fragile, at times fractious, community unsure of their audience. You feel they are in limbo, staring into the void and there is no way back.

A related aspect of Bergman's early infatuation with Nietzsche is a twofold concern with the masks of performance and the aristocracy of the spirit. The central protagonists of *Persona* (Elisabet Vogler) and *Hour of the Wolf* (1967)

(Johan Borg) are self-defining aristocrats of the spirit, high priests of artistic culture whose minds are unhinged and whose powers are undermined and negated. Theirs is a tortuous journey from the aristocratic to the abject, in which their many different masks are stripped away. At the same time both films are two of Bergman's most reflexive: features in which the presence of the camera, as a modern cinematic machine, is most heavily acknowledged. Jean-Luc Godard and Jean-Louis Comolli have both remarked on this shared aspect of the two films – they seem to be *sui generis*, made purely by a camera and not by a director, by a machine and not by human beings (Godard 1986:298; Comolli 1986:315). The powerful paradox of both films as elliptical modernist narratives with uncertain endings is this: their central subjects are aspiring super-humans but their cinematic rendition seems at times to be supra-human. Bergman's demons not only invade the central protagonists but the cinematic machine itself. The impersonal, the automatic, the mechanical, all supreme instances for many critics of 'the death of the subject', are here the very opposite: they simply reinforce his frail yet tangible existence by referring back to the inscrutable demons that torment him. The terror of the auteur is not the death of the auteur, but a form of living death without end, until it is ended by death itself.

The Post-Nietzschean Wager 2: Modernity and Its Demons

When he eventually moved away from Nietzsche, Bergman did so for two reasons: firstly his greater obsession with the demonic over the decadent, and secondly his mature recognition that modern personality was much more complex than Nietzsche gave it credit (Orr 2008:154–55). This leads to a remarkable paradox. It is not true to say that the secular replaces the religious in Bergman's later cinema, any more than it is to say that his apparent embrace of the secular merely hides deeper metaphysical concerns. The truth is that he becomes more secular and more demonic at the same time. By the 1960s, his vision of human complexity and his aesthetics of the face had become a landmark in European film. But as Jacques Aumont has pointed out, the demonic forces that were diluted in his early films intensified with the later ones. *Persona*, *The Rite*, *A Passion* and *Hour of the Wolf* are truly monstrous after the pitiful female demons of Mimi Nelson in *Three Strange Loves* and Margit Carlqvist in *To Joy* (Aumont 2003:109–14). In the age of the welfare state, demons operate at the very heart of bourgeois civility and thrive in the very habitat of reason itself. Bergman's professionals on one view are caring, progressive and rational; on another they incubate the demonic forces that threaten the very fabric of civilization itself. This, as it were, creates a parallax view in which we oscillate back and forth from one intuitive reading to another; readings that should be mutually exclusive but, in Bergman's case, never are. Demonic disorder or secular malaise? Bergman's answer: demonic disorder equals secular malaise. This is the nub of the Swede's modernism and of European modernism in general (Orr 2010). In Bergman's case, philosophical enigma is translated stylistically into forms of concrete abstraction: the intimate drama of the face, its masks and doubles, the white-outs of backdrops, the isolations of geography. Deleuze's any-space-whatever becomes, identifiably, Bergman's any-space-whatever, which may seem to be any-space-whatever but is in truth its opposite, a space selected with great care and attention for its very lack of identification marks. Yet concrete images do haunt us, enduring and vivid – sea and coastline, rock and shore (always), tree and forest (less frequently), the farm or summer house in the middle of nowhere (recurrently). No way in or out, no journey to or from: there-ness is all.

Moreover, there is no psychoanalytic road map, no true 'secular' substitute for the demonic, no Jungian archetypes or Freudian unconscious. Damaged childhood, Oedipus, or the return of the repressed, all offer little illumination in watching his films. But neither, in Bergman's view, are we ever truly rational beings. Paisley Livingston has pointed out a plausible source of Bergman's vision in the writings of Eino Kaila, the Finnish philosopher whose book, *The Psychology of the Personality* (1934), Bergman had acknowledged in 1958 as a vibrant inspiration in his preface to the screenplay of *Wild Strawberries* (Livingston 2008:121). For Bergman, Kaila's insistence on the primacy of need, want and desire – all Anglophone synonyms for the Finnish tarve or the Swedish behov – enabled him to forge a grounded, holistic vision of humans as material beings (ibid.:123–24). Reason is not necessarily the slave of the passions, as Hume tentatively inferred, but very often it can be. For Kaila, the primacy of need can make us delusional, justifying base self-interest as highly moral, and for Bergman, one suspects, his characters interpret something profane as reverentially sacred. Bergman, hence, is not a metaphysical visionary: he is no Dreyer or Tarkovsky. He is always earth-bound in his starting point. His characters may have supernatural visions but he has no such illusions. Kaila also points out a specific form of rationalization that, if we follow Livingston's argument, recurs in Bergman's films – the self-justification of failure. In the traditional fable, the fox who fails to reach the grapes he covets, then reasons ex post facto they are sour. We can take this further. On the rebound from Nietzsche the young Bergman, bruised by his early failures in politics and filmmaking, finally saw that his Nietzschean ideal – ruthless, dynamic striving or impulsion – did not guarantee success; yet to go on living we invent reasons for this shortfall to obviate our humiliation. Self-delusion at times becomes essential to our survival and Bergman becomes a chastened post–Nietzschean artist whose medium, paradoxically, involved a Nietzschean fulfilment.

Bergman's cinema, however, goes far beyond Kaila's insight in one vital respect. It is always a cinema of ludic and emotional encounter, entangled and trans-active. His special insight is that we can often recognize through the power of reasoning, the shortfall of others, while failing to recognize our own. The game we then play is to expose others before they can expose us. Reason, faith, science, psychology, psychoanalysis – all are forms of discourse that double as weapons of power, weapons we can use against others and others can use against us. This is why most of Bergman's major figures are true psychic gladiators, only half-protected by the emblazoned shields of faith or reason. This intimate gladiatorial combat is of course the kind of contest at which Bergman excels, and out of which he forges a special kind of *Kammerspiel* drama. Here, if we can identify the shortcomings of others, it often allows us, conveniently, to ignore our own. Priests and psychiatrists on opposite sides of the secular–religious divide, are nonetheless united by this: their profession demands that they expose weakness in terms of their special language. Sin is sin and guilt is guilt and both are 'moral' failures, revelations of weakness detected through specialist knowledge. Yet as director-writer, pure auteur, posturing as God in his tiny self-created universe, Bergman is also judging those who officially judge. At times his judgments can be pitiless.

If we left things here, we would be defaulting on our own powers of judgment. For Bergman's cinema is also, as we have seen, a cinema of demonic possession in which his modernist turn is not secular at all, but conversely signifies the greater subtlety and greater impact of demons, where many of Bergman's central characters – like those of Dostoevsky – are still 'the possessed'. And possession applies equally to those who are irrational, and those who possess the power of rational judgment. For Bergman, the irrational defiance of rational authority on one side, and the rational 'exposure' of the irrational on the other, can be equally demonic: this is the heart of demonology. It can work through reason just as much as its absence, for if it truly exists, then reason is no barrier against it. The Vergerus characters who recur in different faces and forms throughout his work (in, for example, *The Face, A Passion* and *The Serpent's Egg*) always match the demonic to the rational in ways that are not obvious to us as spectators, or necessarily to them as players in the demonic game. We thus hit upon the supreme contradiction in Bergman's cinema that forges its claim to greatness. He is a demonic materialist. A grounded world gives no credence to metaphysics but, on the other hand, the ostensible triumph of reason cannot eliminate demonic being. On the contrary, the demonic impulse can all too easily swallow up our vulnerable powers of reasoning. Bergman the artist, faced with the great destructiveness of his own century and his youthful delusions about its worst perpetrators, often envisages the Devil as the cunning hand of reason in its most advanced forms. In the nuclear age it remains at the back of our minds a Manichean heresy, at times hard to resist. In most cases we pull ourselves together and shrug it off, banish it to the realm of stupid and unfounded fear. But it is precisely this fear, not fake metaphysics or kitsch neurosis, which gives Bergman's cinema its strength to constantly unsettle us.

The Archipelago Effect: A Reprise

Let us now sum up. As noted, Bergman's early working methods were dictated by the Nordic seasons. At the start of his dual career, he would generally work nine months or so on the stage, then in the late spring and early summer switch to filmmaking, often to make use of the summer light of the Stockholm archipelago, seen in the four distinctive films he made at the start of the 1950s: *To Joy, Summer Interlude, Waiting Women* and most famously *Summer with Monika*. The power of topographical escape is everywhere in these pictures. It was not only escape from a gloomy Stockholm, a city that Bergman claimed he detested in winter, but also a reinstatement of something he had left out of his ongoing pastiche of poetic realism – the fugitive theme. The 1940s films were inert, studio-bound, full of bickering couples and existential angst with the density of treacle. Lorens Marmstedt, the producer of the modest and small-scale company Terrafilm, who took over much of his earlier work and often acted as a reality check on Bergman's ambition, had to remind the director that his actor pal, Birger Malmsten was no Jean Gabin and he was no Marcel Carné (Bergman 1995:132). With no Gabin, Bergman had no real feel for the dynamic movement of the fugitive thriller, or its criminality, which British films – *Odd Man Out* (1947), *They Made Me a Fugitive*

(1947) and *The Third Man* (1949) – had taken over from the French so effectively in the postwar years.

Apart from the flawed and fascinating criminal, that pre-war Gabin and postwar British film had fashioned so brilliantly, the other notable absence in the 1950s is Bergman's studied evasion of the dilemma of the aspiring male artist. There was, in effect, no substantial Portrait of the Artist as a Young Man. Straight autobiography was largely off limits. If anything, the artistic figures within Bergman's films were female, dancers and musicians. Indeed the artificiality of Bergman's young males in much of his early work is highlighted by the authentic look and feel of Bo Widerberg's *Raven's End*, made in 1963 with improved film technologies no doubt, but with a precision, depth of feeling and intense focus on the uncertainties of its young male hero that early Bergman had lacked. Widerberg's black and white film, enduringly popular with Swedish audiences and a personal favourite of Bergman himself, recreated the austerity of 1930s Malmö with atmospheric location shooting and a sense of time and place that the early Bergman had never shown. Widerberg's aspiring young writer Anders, played so well by Thommy Berggren, whom Bergman tried and failed to entice into his own films (Koskinen, 2010:33–34), is trapped in a bleak workers' apartment with his alcoholic father and suffering mother and is patronized by a Stockholm publisher who plays humiliating games with him. Anders gets his girlfriend pregnant and finally makes his escape from the city, leaving all behind. The sense of early art-humiliation that Bergman discusses in his memoir seems exemplified here more than anywhere in Swedish film. To be sure Bergman came partly cushioned from a middle-class family and this is much bleaker, more proletarian; but the film is also more lyrical and more passionate about this predicament than Bergman could ever be. For male heroism, however flawed, Bergman works instead through displacement instead of autobiography. Thus his great male heroes of the 1950s are a medieval knight and an ageing university professor. His late encounter with the male artist comes in the modernist fable of the late 1960s *Hour of the Wolf*, where Bergman gives us a contemporary portrait of the tormented male artist, but also in a way that is quite pitiless and oblique, producing one of his greatest films.

As someone who could never make a naturalistic film as austerely beautiful as *Raven's End*, Bergman had hit on an alternate strategy. He sidelined Malmsten and invented the archipelago escape as an escape into romance, feminizing its protagonists: the desiring woman replaced Gabin's running man as Maj-Britt Nilsson and Harriet Andersson made their mark as love-fugitives on island locations, trying to escape family and convention. In its day, Andersson's Monika was a shock to the system in the film's final act of leaving spouse and child, Bergman's sharp and demonic update on Nora Helmer in *A Doll's House*, which he was to direct so brilliantly for the stage with Pernilla August late in life. And the Swede had his own variation on the Ibsen theme. Monika flees twice over: in the first act from the dreary workplace and family home in austere Stockholm, abandoned for a lover's flight; and in the final act, lover and child are abandoned in a shoddy apartment for a second journey into dubious freedom – a true Bergman provocation, left open. And when Bergman saw Fellini's 1954 *La Strada* a revelation was at hand (Aghed 2007:193). The performing tradition he had used in *Sawdust and Tinsel* need not be so heavy and expressionistic. It could embody the lyricism of pure movement on open landscapes, and the momentum of the road movie could flesh out the abstraction of Strindberg's dream journey. *The Seventh Seal, The Face* and *Wild Strawberries* were soon to follow.

With *Monika*, Bergman had made a breakthrough of sorts. He made his own special nod to the art of moviemaking too, soon to make him a darling of the Nouvelle Vague; or rather halfway through the film Monika had made him so, turning sensuously and slowly round from profile towards full face, staring directly at us all. It was his first act of full-frontal spectator seduction, and you suspect that Bergman had long craved to perfect it in his tussle with the art of the moving image. We, the audience, are now hooked and implicated, but also challenged. Are we right to be enchanted by a treacherous girl who is about to return to an abusive lover? For her director, it was the end of an agonizing apprenticeship, the very opposite of Hollywood boy wonder Orson Welles, who had astonished the film world in his debut, *Citizen Kane* (1941), only to lose his way in Tinseltown and then be banished. For Bergman, it was after ten long, tortuous years in movie directing, with his twentieth feature, that he at last got near to the universal acclaim he was seeking: critical and commercial, home and abroad. And he did this with a comedy. His elegant costume drama *Smiles of a Summer Night* won the Special Jury Prize for 1956 at Cannes. It had been a long night's journey into day, as *Daybreak* (1939), the Carné film Bergman had endlessly failed to remake, gave way at last to a real daybreak. And from then on there was no turning back. Writer of his own screenplays, begetter of original projects, Bergman become one the truly great artists of European cinema.

More than this however, he went on to forge a cinema that took him out of the periphery of European cinema and into its very core. Geographically isolated in his repeated locations in the Stockholm archipelago, on the shores of southern Sweden and in remote Fårö, he was to change the face of European cinema, setting a template for those who directed on location in suburbs and cities. Battling with faith, he inspired others who battled with faith and in turn was inspired by them. Probing the fragile nature of European civilization, he was a model for others who sought to do likewise. And amid the grand solemnity that has often been linked in a facile way to lofty metaphysical questions, he had been refreshingly down to earth in displaying the grounded, performative, and often comic aspects of modernity. A host of European names can be framed around him, all in some way his creative equals – predecessors, contemporaries, successors, Lang, Dreyer, Godard and the French New Wave, Fellini and Antonioni, Wajda and Kieslowski, Tarkovsky, Von Trier, Haneke – and many others. To reinstate Bergman within this wider spectrum when he has often been seen as isolated, divorced, apart, is the purpose of the rest of this book.

CHAPTER TWO

The Shadow of Transcendence
Dreyer–Bergman–Tarkovsky

In cinema transcendence is two things. It is surpassing, of the limits and boundaries of the life-world: a mode of surpassing pronounced by religious faith, political utopia, visions of the supernatural and extra sensory perception. It is also transfiguration: a miraculous transformation on screen of the human image where none seems possible – in short a resurrection. In this respect Bergman's films are seldom transcendental: they probe the very boundaries and limits of the life-world and question what is beyond relentlessly, but in vain. They are on the rebound from the effort of surpassing and no resurrection seems possible. Yet they do shadow transcendence elsewhere. That 'elsewhere' in European cinema lies, most notably, in the films of Carl Theodor Dreyer and Andrei Tarkovsky. Uncannily, Bergman's cinema seems to shadow their 'elsewhere' cinema – to be its material antiphon. Two alternate tropes emerge here: the transcendental figure without the earthly shadow (Dreyer, Tarkovsky), or the earthly shadow of transcendence without the transcendental figure (Bergman). To say also that Bergman 'shadows' Dreyer and later Tarkovsky is to speak metaphorically. But the process embedded beneath these metaphors is metonymic. In Dreyer and Tarkovsky the very act of filming often seems to intimate the existence of another world besides the life-world, so there is not just a double but a triple layering, not just the interplay between the life-world and the world of film but a triangulation of life-world, film world and transcendental world.

Yet for Bergman, the transcendental is across the line, always on the other side of the life-world and the film world – invisible, silent, unknown – just as Karin's God-spider in *Through a Glass Darkly* is on the other side of her bedroom wall. Only the delusions of madness bring it through the wall. In Dreyer and Tarkovsky, on the other hand, the transcendental vision goes beyond the life-world and beyond madness, even when the harbinger of the vision – Johannes in *Ordet* (1955) or Andrei Rublev for example – may be considered mad by others, including the spectator. In European cinema too, transcendence has had its own special form of surplus value that cannot be referred to pure metaphysics: the birth, death and rebirth of Christianity. Dreyer brought it into the film world, Bergman agonized over its impending death, Pasolini merged the gospel according to Matthew with the gospel according to Marx, and Tarkovsky in a Soviet society declared officially atheist, used cinema as the chosen medium of Orthodox Christian resurrection.

There are of course differences. Dreyer and Bergman share the legacy of Nordic Protestantism: its Lutheran piety and the provocative writings of Kierkegaard. Tarkovsky sources the divine iconography of the Russian Orthodox, buried during his career beneath geological layers of Marxist-Leninism. And there are key differences between Dreyer and Bergman. One was a maker of very few features in the sound era, the other a maker of several dozen. From early on Dreyer made films in France, Sweden and Germany as well as Denmark; Bergman came to Germany very late on, after leaving Sweden feeling hounded by the Swedish tax authorities and the media (Bergman 1988:102). It is possible to argue about whether Dreyer was a Danish director first and a European one second, or vice versa. Yet with Bergman there seems little point. Bar two, all his films were Swedish, and by choice. Yet there is a common legacy. The silent films of Mauritz Stiller, Victor Sjöström and German Expressionism all left their indelible mark. And both directors planned to film a life of Jesus – Dreyer in great detail: plans that never came to fruition. Dreyer's silent 1928 classic *The Passion of Joan of Arc* was one of Bergman's favourite films and provides us with a key starting point. In Bergman's later portfolio, this film bifurcates in its afterlife (the world of sound) into the equally medieval *Seventh Seal* and the equally bold staging of facial abstraction that is very contemporary – *Persona*. It thus percolates into both the romantic-classical and modernist dimensions of Bergman's cinema. Like *Day of Wrath* (1943) and *Ordet*, it foregrounds the heroine, the female protagonist, which is what Bergman did recurrently from *Summer Interlude* onwards. The physiognomy of the face becomes the physiognomy of the woman's face: generically transcendental in the images of Dreyer, generically material in the images of Bergman, enigmatic in both. It is of course more than a matter of degree. In Dreyer the uplifted face of suffering faces mortality but intimates the Beyond: in Bergman the perplexed face of suffering intimates mortality and fails to surpass it, to find the Beyond it often craves. Before we trace this Bergmanesque process in all its distinctive variations – the process of unsurpassing – let us turn to the more specific legacy of Dreyer.

For Hamlet, Shakespeare's Danish Prince, famously 'the time is out of joint': for the Danish Dreyer, a maverick figure in European cinema for over thirty years, all space is out of joint. Aumont points out that, like Antonioni and Straub after him,

Dreyer's film style is based on, 'a deliberate and active decentring, usually aiming to emphasise certain expressive values of the frame' (Aumont 1997:115). It makes no conventional attempt to naturalize space either in staging or editing, because for Dreyer our normal spatial perceptions are themselves restricting and misleading. How for example do the human senses 'perceive' that centrepiece of Einsteinian relativity – four-dimensional space? The truth is they cannot: something more is needed. After filming *Ordet* in 1954, Dreyer claimed the new science had not only unfolded the relativity of time as the fourth dimension, but also a fifth dimension: the psychical, where it was possible to experience things that had not yet taken place. Thus he spoke of a 'deep connection between exact science and intuitive religion' (Dreyer 1973:164), where science can furnish a deeper understanding of the divine. In this film Dreyer is both highly archaic and very contemporary: his family's traditional farmhouse is the locus of stylistic simplicity, and yet also the sacred site of the concluding miracle; such that essentialist style and essential miracle, the miracle of resurrection, merge into one, exonerating each other. Much earlier, after the release of *Joan*, he used a different term to express the role of the human face in the revelation of this potential merger: 'realised mysticism'(ibid.:50). It is a blend of 'realised mysticism' and the 'fifth dimension' that forms Dreyer's vision of the transcendental, the filmic expression of the Beyond on the canvas of everyday life.

What Dreyer saw as realized mysticism, Bergman reworked as mystified reality; one Nordic artist fascinated by the realization of the mystical in the moving image, the other by its role in the cultural mystification of the real. If there is a call and response effect in their relationship, it is scarcely conscious and it is framed by the Lutheran faith common to their life-worlds. We can see therefore in *The Seventh Seal* and *Persona* schizophrenic alternatives to *Joan* – one set in time past, the other in time present. We can see in the passion subplot of *Smiles of a Summer Night*, concerning the young wife Anne Egerman and her devout stepson Henrik, a comic response to the doomed, tragic passion of *Day of Wrath*. And there is a bleak yet very atmospheric alternative to the 'resurrection' that ends *Ordet* in *Winter Light* (1963), in which death prevails and there are no miracles at all. If the vampirism of Dreyer's *Vampyr* (1932) takes us both literally and metaphorically beyond the grave into the world of the undead, *Persona* brings it back from the dead and its Gothic symbols of death. Bergman's vampirism is no longer the attribute of possessed supernatural 'creatures' but the form of a perverse intimacy, a psychic act of devouring. Though their careers overlap, we can note a pattern to cinematic evolution and pass from Dreyer's filmic schema or paradigm to Bergman's paradigm by way of Dreyer, and later pass from Bergman's visionary form to Tarkovsky's visionary form – by way of Bergman. If Dreyer strives for the transcendental, then Bergman literally unsurpasses, only for Tarkovsky to resurrect the filmic moment of surpassing in a different setting, a different culture, a different country.

The decentring of space in Dreyer's *Joan* begins with the faces at Joan's trial, including her own, where she so often occupies the edge of the frame. The judges are placed unnaturally high above her, so that her upward gaze can be construed in two ways: as confused and deferential or as seeking to gaze through and beyond; gaze upward, that is, towards the invisible that is masked by the blank white spaces of the Dreyer background, where the gaze must penetrate both the blocking heads and the whiteness of abstraction behind them. Before Hollywood's decade of talking heads, Dreyer provides us with something else: the floating heads of patriarchy with disembodied faces that block Joan's transcendental vision, while their discourse is its verbal correlative, its array of lip movements demanding retraction of the heresy of her personal visions of the Lord, of the divine visions and voices that urged her to fight the English. While the floating heads often appear around the edges of the frame in mismatched cuts, they use their silent mouthing voices to demand confession: their faces sneer in condescension at the young naïf before them. Facing down at her formidably, in a montage of high-angle shots, the collective patriarchy are a collection of grotesques and gargoyles admonishing an errant child. But the face of Falconetti as Joan more than answers them, since it consistently embodies suffering and vision at the same time, and never one to the detriment of the other. Moreover, it never succumbs to the pressure, to the retreat of downcast eyes. It absorbs the suffering that public humiliation creates but gazes back, beyond the neutral canvas of the blank white walls behind the floating heads, upward towards eternity. Dreyer rigorously avoids in his many reverse angles the obvious point-of-view shot for his heroine. The faces confronting her are not centred on her vision but somehow adrift in space; they float free, anywhere and nowhere at the same time. A reverse angle is thus not a reaction shot as it is in the lexicon of classical narration. Dreyer's camera itself seems adrift in space, as if defying gravity.

If at the trial, all space is out of joint, this is a pointer to moral malfunctioning: the judgment on Joan is wrong, unjust, unjustifiable. Dreyer's cinematic staging is not just a modernist technique – which it clearly is – but a moral statement, in which the actor creates a special state of being. As Dreyer said apropos of Falconetti, it is realized mysticism through the performance of a great historical figure – what he termed 'the martyr's reincarnation' (Dreyer 1973:50). The moving image and film performance in their purest form bring the martyr back from the dead annals of history. With Dreyer we are always close, often unbearably so, to the 'passion' of his subject, all the way to the final burning at the stake where his Joan still remains a revered figure among the French populace. Bergman's stake-burning in *The Seventh Seal* is fascinating because it seems at the opposite end of the spectrum. His female victim is no longer subject but object, not a national martyr but a young local 'witch'; her fate a passing distraction to the blonde knight Antonius Block as he pursues his fruitless journey of divine illumination in plague-ridden Sweden. Falconetti's eyes burn with the conviction of rectitude and vision, but her Swedish double is more often seen from afar, her eyes full of anguish but her nature unknown until she confirms to Block, before her burning, the charge against her of consorting with the devil. She proudly confesses the special relationship with the Evil One of which she is accused, just as Anne at the end of *Day of Wrath* had turned the accusation of witchcraft into a positive affirmation of selfhood and passionate love. Exhausted by seeking out an elusive God who remains silent and hidden, Block momentarily succumbs to the temptation of seeking out the proximate devil: the girl is cast as an intermediary, the demonic a passing sign of the transcendental. But the young 'witch' knows what she knows in her own mind, a link that is a special gift, an exclusive provenance. She has faith in her vision of the Evil One, while Block no longer has faith in the existence of God, and her eyes at the end are a mixture of defiance and fear. In her final moments, she still has something Block does not – demonic presence. And Block knows he still has nothing but sacred absence. Resigned, he abandons her to her fate.

A decade prior to *The Seventh Seal*, Dreyer of course had produced his own witch-burning, the persecution of the ageing Herlof's Marte at the start of the seventeenth-century *Day of Wrath*. The implication at the end is that newly-wed Anne Pedersson, played brilliantly by Lisbeth Movin, will suffer the same fate. Dreyer poises things perfectly. Anne's mother has earlier narrowly evaded the accusation of witchcraft. Is the accusation of Anne merely a continuation of unjust persecution, or a genuine bloodline that makes her a demonic figure? Is the radiance of Anne's gaze a sign of transcendent godliness or of demonic possession? Dreyer forces his audience to choose and in doing so to confront their own prejudices and suspicions. Bergman's medieval 'witch' repeats the dilemma in a minor key. Has the local girl in the Swedish forest internalized the accusation of having carnal intercourse with the Devil, then proudly and perversely accepted it; or is she simply an innocent victim of desperate men seeking remedies to the ravages of the plague? But if this echoes in passing the ambiguities of Dreyer's more complex discourse, Bergman, again in a minor key, sought to transform tragedy into comedy where Lutheran morality flies out of the window. In *Smiles of a Summer Night*, which celebrates the start of the twentieth century, he creates another stepmother Anne, young Anne Egerman instead of young Anne Pedersson, and inverts the tragic dilemma of *Day of Wrath* within the hedonistic circles of the Swedish rich. Unlike stern clergyman Absalon Pedersson, husband–father Fredrik Egerman is a wealthy philandering lawyer intent on regaining his old actress-flame, while his son in revolt is a devout, despairing theology student tortured by the temptations of the flesh. Like several of Bergman's characters he contemplates suicide, but fails in his resolve quite hilariously as the director plays despair for laughs. Unlike Dreyer's Anne, whose brazen confession of adultery drives her shocked husband to a fatal seizure, Bergman's Anne – a virgin bride – is fresh-faced innocence personified. In 1955, Bergman's affectionate lampooning of Lutheranism was an inside job; while in 1943 Dreyer, under the shadow of German occupation, had still been wrestling with its seventeenth century legacy. The Swedish film is a comic triumph, just as the Danish film had been a tragic masterpiece. Yet the fertility of Bergman's reinvention after the genius of Dreyer's invention, change of genre plus schema with variation that continually surprises, remains one the high points of Nordic cinema. Both in their own terms are equally convincing, each a cinematic triumph.

Natural Born Vampires: *Vampyr* and *Persona*

Comparing these two complex films that are spaced over thirty years apart, we find an inverse symmetry between life and art. After the release of *Vampyr* in 1932, Dreyer had a severe breakdown. Before the writing of *Persona*, Bergman had his own (less serious) crack-up (Björkman et al. 1973:195–8). In one case, we might say the efforts of art generated madness; in the other, the prospect of madness prompted escape into art. Dreyer's career went into lockdown, while Bergman's film inaugurated in 1966 his most inventive ten years in a prolific career. For many viewers, the two films remain the most baffling and enigmatic in their respective repertoires. How to read them? With unreliable prints in different languages, *Vampyr* was largely forgotten. With greater availability and better technology, *Persona* was endlessly discussed. Both films disorient our sense of chronology, of continuity, of meaning, of the relationship between space and time. One appears on the cusp of early modernism, as film makes the transfer from silence to sound. It stands out in the European modernism of the age, alongside *Un Chien Andalou* (1928), *L'Âge d'or* (1930), *The Blood of a Poet* (1930), *M* (1931) and *Blackmail* (1929). In the neo-modern renaissance of the 1960s, where modernism makes its great return, *Persona* in turn stands out alongside *8½* (1963), *Pierrot le fou* (1965), *Muriel* (1963), *Belle de jour* (1967) and *Red Desert* (1964). Both are enigmatic, yet both are markers of a broader artistic triumph. And with the return of modernism, we can also detect in the close relationship of Dreyer and Bergman a more muted trope, the Return of the Vampire.

While Dreyer's vampirism was announced in his film's title, Bergman's is anything but obvious. Dreyer was aiming to make a commercial film within a successful genre; Bergman was aiming to make his audience sit through a feature with effectively only two characters, both of them women. It was to be the most intense and intimate of all his chamber films. The differences are vast. *Vampyr* has a list of characters who suddenly appear out of nowhere to the bemused Allan Grey and are unexplained, often as shadows or reflections without bodies before they assume human form. The shoot used found locations north of Paris: a local inn that turns into a spatial labyrinth, a derelict factory, a crumbling chateau. A tight budget meant no studio builds, no artificial design, no special effects, no contrived signs of the supernatural; for Dreyer there is no divide between the natural and supernatural. The natural is the supernatural. Humans, vampires and vampire victims intermingle and are interchangeable figures in the panoramic canvas of the undead. Landscapes are pastoral and Gothic at the same time; buildings are naturalistic and Gothic at the same time. Destruction of space–time coordinates on location is the order of the day, but exclusively through the natural image. Dreyer's Gothic modernism is, in 1932, already post-expressionist, not using artificial distortion of the image to induce menace; but the spatial disjunctions between cutting and camera movement that destroy eyeline matches, distance continuities, the 180-degree axis and any sense of direction the spectator might have. If the bewildered Grey does not know who he sees or where exactly he is, then neither do we. Yet this is not pure subjective fantasy, the desperation of a demented mind. The camera frequently abandons his bewildered eye because it has a life and momentum of its own. It often seems as if it too, our trusted medium of the objective, is baffled by events in spite of its 'objective' power; in spite, that is, of the advantage it has over its protagonist. Not only is there no clear dividing line between the subjective and the objective in this film: there is no sense either in which one has a perceptual advantage over the other.

With its dazzling prologue montage that simulates the birth of the film inside its projector, *Persona* seems to echo *Vampyr's* initial narrative confusion. But after that its narrative poetics go in the opposite direction and restore meaning immediately. The film places and positions its characters for us through its third-person narration and psychiatric diagnoses. We are told that Elisabet Vogler is a celebrity actress married with a young child and that Sister Alma has been designated to care for her after Vogler's breakdown onstage in a performance of *Electra*. The actress laughs in the middle of classical tragedy, then refuses to speak and, dumbstruck, has not spoken since. Having thrown us initially with the birthing of the film as the birth of cinema itself, Bergman thus restores our coordinates in the story of the film. We sense a suspense story will unfold when the woman psychiatrist offers Elisabet and her new nurse her coastal summer house as a place for rest and recuperation (though the 'offer' is in essence an order). Cut to Bergman's location shots on Fårö and we are squarely placed in position: the summer house, the isolation, the bare landscapes, the sea and shore. Will Sister Alma nurse the mute Elisabet back to health and back to speech? Or will she fail? But then we expect other characters to enter and deepen the story. With the brief exception of Elisabet's husband, in a scene that could well be a dream, none do. What then is happening?

Like the hospital sequence, Bergman is clearly using the summer house interiors (shot on location in Fårö) to create a specific ambience (Björkman et al. 1973:203). In terms of staging, both sets of interiors fold over fluidly, one into the other: bare white walls, gauze curtains, rectangularity, minimal furniture, ample spaces, the clean lines of modernist design with no adornment. The abstraction is near theatrical but also reminiscent in its designed simplicity of the bare rectangular patterns of the family farmhouse in *Ordet*, now updated to the age of the summer house and the welfare state. In both *Ordet* and *Persona* the interior setting is stripped to essentials. A specific sequence from *Vampyr* may also have inspired Bergman in establishing the relation of the two women. From her sickbed Léone dominates both her younger sister Gisèle and her uniformed nurse after she has been bitten and infected by Marguerite Chopin, the ageing cemetery vampire we view only from afar. For Dreyer the source of evil, Chopin, is confined largely to long shot: her infected victim Leone develops no fangs or sharpened finger nails but her dying is filmed in the emotional desperation of disturbed close-up. As Rudkin notes, Dreyer relies here on the pure acting power of Sybille Schmitz, dwelling in close shot 'on the naked landscape of her face' as she becomes 'a dark martyr sister' to his earlier Joan of Arc (Rudkin 2005:58–59). Thus in the Schmitz performance, her face changes from warm luminosity to extreme desperation, from soft puckered lips to the open baring of the teeth, intense delirium finally conveyed by a fanatical grin. Her carers are alarmed and terrified as if she controls them from her deathbed. In Bergman's film, the active carer Alma, who starts in nursing uniform, seems a composite of Léone's dual carers – Gisèle and the family nurse – and Elisabet is an update of Léone with a difference: she is a cunning performer who through the nuance of the look or expression controls her carer from the sickbed. Thus *Persona* uses the twentieth-century discourse of psychiatric healing to naturalize the vampire trope. This is a secular and rational process of cure. But the film then poses the question: who is curing whom? Here Elisabet's strategy of silence becomes truly fascinating. The silent patient soon leaves her sickbed and dominates the talkative nurse: the summer stay elicits long confessions from the carer, not the patient. And instead of the talking cure, the spoken word signifies a growing departure from sanity – the growing madness of the carer as 'the patient' becomes calculating and sane.

Two wide-shot sequences show the power of performance, and both are virtuoso dumbshows: the staging of mimed performances. In her hospital room, filmed in long shot, Elisabet looks across a bare minimalist space to a flickering television in the far corner. On the screen we see images from war-torn Vietnam, culminating in the public suicide of a Buddhist monk who has set fire to his petrol-soaked clothes. After a moment's hesitation she reacts in fear and then terror, reeling backward and uttering a silent scream. At first sight, this is a sick nervous patient no longer immune to proximate violence on a television screen. It is rendered by Ullmann as mute raw emotion, but at second sight it could well be the seasoned enactment of a clever actress simulating raw emotion, rehearsing for a role to come. Later in the island summerhouse she 'performs' the opposite state of being: pure serenity. Just before dawn she enters Alma's room to awaken the sleeping nurse, pulls her into an affectionate embrace and stands beside her before a mirror to match their faces, suggesting near-perfect resemblance. The drapes in front of the windows filter down the emerging light. The room seems unnaturally wide, just like the hospital room, as if it were a mini stage and Vogler's performance, complete with dramatic entrance, seems a theatrical tour de force. But this time Bergman cuts to close shot to film the two women: the camera is now 'onstage', unbearably close, tensely intimate. We have made the transition this time around, through the intimacy of close shot, from theatre-goers to film spectators. As if to enforce the point, the next sequence is outside, as we pass abruptly from close-up to long shot, the rock-strewn shore filmed in a fixed shot with Alma in the far distance. Elisabet suddenly rises up unexpectedly from the bottom of the frame to look straight at us and block our gaze, then photograph the movie camera, and by implication the spectator. We are implicated, that is to say, by the reflexive pose that heralds the act of filming itself. First turning the world internally into a stage, Elisabet then transforms it externally into a film within a film. Devoid of speech, the vampire devours and dominates through the medium of the visual.

At the start of the film, the brief role of the woman doctor – Margaretha Krook had previously played a hospital doctor for Bergman in *Brink of Life* (1958) – seems straightforward but is anything but. Her judgment on Elisabet seems cruel yet perceptive, her actions rational, embedded in a psychiatric discourse of cause and cure. Her white hospital coat suggests a white-out of personal qualities. Yet like most of Bergman's later portrayals of the caring profession, she is suspect in her judgment. The summerhouse *diktat*, disguised as an invitation, makes her a sinister figure only on second sight: it may be speculation to see her as one of Bergman's post-expressionist demons, as Aumont does (2003) – a scientific demon instigating big mischief, malignly disrupting the order of things while ostensibly advocating reason, cure and compassion. Yet the chaos her judgment precipitates, suggests the speculation is not far from the mark. At times Elisabet does seem like a devil's emissary, marked by neurotic illness and executing demonic experiments. Comparison of Bergman's doctor with Dreyer's demon doctor in *Vampyr* looms large. Yet Dreyer is explicit and melodramatic. Making a late entry to visit the ailing Léone, and then demanding a blood donation from the bemused Allan Grey suggests no demonic masking at all. We have seen him briefly with the village vampire and very soon he becomes a larger-than-life villain, following in the Weimar-canon footsteps of Doctors Caligari and Mabuse. The uncanny difference perhaps is that he looks like an ageing Albert Einstein, that mastermind whose fourth dimension intrigued and disturbed Dreyer so much. If so, he could well be a 'space' impresario stage-managing the severe disjunctions of *chronos* and *topos* in the images that have all but done for the tail-chasing Grey. Dreyer's film then becomes less about the hounding of vampires than the overcoming of relativity. Under the guise of collecting blood, Dreyer's doctor swallows up the common-sense perception of space and leaves Grey to negotiate a nightmare labyrinth. *Persona* is very different. Under the guise of sucking Alma's blood, which at one point Elisabet does from the nurse's forearm, she devours her victim's soul and assumes her face and, still silent, reduces her speech to gibberish. This, for an actress facing the void, is the ultimate form of nourishment. Space, face and soul – these are the vampirisms of twentieth-century abstraction, concepts made viscid through the medium of blood.

While Grey eventually resists the leeching of his powers of perception, to which he at first succumbs in passive delirium, Sister Alma eventually resists the appropriation of her persona: the identity grab to which she at first succumbs in the swoon of heroine worship. Alma craves the image of the stage idol: the celebrity actress with whom she has fallen in love but in whom she then comes, bit by bit, to recognize the cruelty, cynicism and contempt that lie behind the Vogler predation. Both women endure sacrificial acts of humiliation to survive the island and return to the mainland. But while Dreyer opts for romance as Grey and Gisèle head off in mist-strewn pastures, Bergman's ending is at best a damning stalemate: Elisabet goes back to performance, but most likely Alma's self is irreparably damaged. It can be said that in *Vampyr* and *Persona* the *chronos* of film language goes in opposite directions. From its inception *Vampyr* has a technical aesthetic of disorienting, which Grey overcomes only by the superhuman act of 'seeing' through the glass partition of his coffin in the film's most notorious sequence, going further into the world of the undead in order to undermine it. After its baffling prologue, act one of *Persona* is a model of ambiguous clarity, but after the splitting of the reel that conveys Alma's growing anger, act two disintegrates space and time in the attempt to convey the impossible – the act of psychic implosion that defies all film language and cannot finally be read with any conviction at all. In the fractious encounter of the two women that marks the second part of *Persona*, we can see Bergman's camera as a Hadron Collider trying to split the subatomic particles of mind, the basic elements of consciousness previously unknown to us. If Bergman's protagonists all hit a brick wall in their search for transcendence, then Bergman's critics all hit a brick wall in trying to read this film. As *Vampyr* emerges finally into the light, *Persona* delves further into inner darkness and here there is no limit to what Bergman can do. His true claim to transcendence thus lies within the film medium itself. He transcends the limitations of the film world because he can never transcend the world beyond it.

Miracle/No Miracle: *Ordet* and *Winter Light*

Both these films would usually be classified as 'religious', the kind of films classical Hollywood would never really touch. Both deal not just with Christian ministries in trouble, but faith itself in trouble. Dreyer adapts Kaj Munk's family drama about schism and uncertainty in 1920s Denmark: his resolution is transcendental and healing. Conversely, Bergman's contemporary film set in 1962 offers no resolution at all. Life goes on meagre and diminished in what is the most austere of all his features, a state where visual austerity assumes a perverse purity in its execution. In Dreyer, film intimates through Inger's final resurrection the transcendence of the dying body and the troubled soul: in Bergman, film intimates nothing except perhaps God's silence. The body dies, the soul remains troubled. In Dreyer's ending the maternal body is resurrected from the dead: in Bergman's ending there is merely the beginning of the next service in the next church. After death by suicide, bleak November goes on in the forests and hamlets of northern Sweden. From all this it is possible to guess which film is the more heart-warming, but also which is perhaps a more accurate register of the modern soul in Bergman's lifetime. *Ordet* is the luminous persistence of wishful vision; *Winter Light* an acerbic depiction that contains no vision at all, except the disenchantment of life grimly and tenaciously going on. Chronology may help to explain things since *Ordet* (1955) precedes *Winter Light* (1963) by eight long years. In one sense, Dreyer's film has more in common with other 1950s miracle films such as Rossellini's *Voyage to Italy* (1953) and Hitchcock's *The Wrong Man* (1956). In another sense however, *Winter Light* is its prodigal offspring, closer by being further away, not so much schema through variation, which Cousins (2004: 326) suggests is the normal pattern of film evolution, but as schema through extreme deviation, yet still perversely *en famille*. Seen in the twenty-first century, the gap between them seems to stretch out for much more than eight years. Set in 1925, *Ordet* is uncannily archaic; while set in 1962, *Winter Light*, with its ambient fear of nuclear war, is more acutely contemporary. And yet *Ordet* remains hypnotic, compelling and dare we say it, the unofficial bible of Lars von Trier. And what in the age of *Antichrist* (2009) is more contemporary than that?

Often the triumph of film form lies in a seamless fusion of style and theme. This, it has to be said, is true of both these films. Dreyer matches the long take and the medium-long shot to his search for spiritual unity. Bergman uses close shots, extreme long shots, reverse angles and separation through editing to indicate distance and breakdown. Dreyer's close-knit protagonists argue about meaning and dogma but finally pull together. Bergman's lonely communicants skirt around their feelings and differences and finally move apart. It is not then a matter of proclaiming the triumph of Dreyer over Bergman because of his impressive average shot length and his mastery of what he called, 'a continuous, flowing, horizontally gliding motion' in his films (Dreyer 1973:129). The long take, like the reverse angle, performs a task for Dreyer and can be admired for doing so. It is a technique of unfolding, of moving the eye horizontally since as Dreyer points out, 'the eye is involuntarily attracted by objects in motion but remains passive over stationary things' (ibid.). Movement through space precipitates the possibilities of transcending. Bergman on the other hand, is the maestro of the still shot, the visual freezing of the moment when the soul reveals itself through the proximity of the body, through voice, gesture and in close-up, the enigmas of the human face. Dreyer's camera transforms the frame: Bergman's camera explores it: brilliantly so as he cuts swiftly from Pastor Tomas reading Märta's imploring letter, to a sustained long take where Märta recites it straight to camera in close-up and the spectator has nowhere to hide. This choice between stillness and movement reverberates through film history, not only Bergman versus Dreyer but equally Ozu versus Mizoguchi, Bresson versus Tarkovsky, Kiarostami versus Angelopoulos. It is a choice in which finally we do not have to choose at all. Cinema flourishes in the endless play of opposites, and that is why we can place *Ordet* and *Winter Light* side by side as films that can both explore the dilemmas of Nordic Protestantism in the twentieth century and yet be completely different films, which at the same time are universal through the precision and detail in their vision of the human condition.

A question posed by these two films that results in different answers is the following: what constitutes the site of the sacred? In *Ordet* it is the patriarchal home set amid the dunes: the traditional Jutland farmhouse of the Borgen family, where pain, conflict and finally miracle are acted out; whereas in *Winter Light*, it is the country Uppland church that is the central arena of human drama. Dreyer transforms the everyday home into the site of the sacred, while Bergman turns the sacred site, the place of worship, into the domain of the profane, where fraught personal crises predominate. The inversion is near symmetrical. Dreyer's characters never step into an official place of worship, while Pastor Tomas Ericsson (Gunnar Björnstrand) never steps into anyone's home, including his own. This avoidance of home-ness is stressed twice. When he has to inform Karin Persson (Gunnel Lindblom) of her husband's suicide, he steps briefly into her hallway but not into the living room where she has to tell her children the tragic news. He merely stares at them through the front window as he makes a swift departure. When he accepts an invitation from his lover, schoolteacher Märta Lundberg (Ingrid Thulin), to her home, he diverts her to the adjacent schoolhouse to avoid Märta's aunt, who is staying for tea. They talk briefly, surrounded by school desks. Every Ericsson setting is institutional, even the outside scene of the suicide by the roaring rapids, where the police have got there first to investigate and cover over Jonas Persson's dead body. The film begins at midday with Tomas conducting church communion and ends three hours later with him starting to conduct a service in another church. Where is home?

The Borgen farmhouse is not only the site of the sacred but also of the uncanny, homeliness made strange through its absorption of the universal, as if it compressed the world's drama into its tight horizontal frame. It also has to accommodate the unexpected entrances and exits of the deranged Johannes, the prodigal son who enters the frame out of nowhere and vanishes just as swiftly. In the naturalistic studio design for his Uppland churches, Bergman takes the opposite route. Their vast height and depth and stark minimalism dwarf their meagre handful of worshippers; but there is no interior adornment to offer solace or belonging, no symbolism save that of the crucified saviour dying on the cross in agony. The communion ceremony is formal and distant, the church freezing in early winter, all human warmth gone as ice grips the soul. In *Ordet* the warmth of the home and the reconciliation of religious differences prompted by Inger's death act as vital conditions for her miraculous rebirth; but in *Winter Light* the absence of warmth and reassurance, the abject failure of Pastor Tomas in his duties of pastoral care, accelerates the motion of Jonas, gripped by his fear of nuclear war, towards an untimely death. Inger's death occurs through 'natural' causes, her resurrection through the miracle of faith. The death of Jonas occurs courtesy of his own rifle and there is no miracle of faith to resurrect his crumpled corpse. Inger is laid to rest, serene in medium shot in her immaculate coffin, a beautiful body waiting to be reborn. Filmed in long shot, the dead Jonas looks like a bundle of rags spread out by a riverside in winter – identification marks none.

The key figures of middle brother Johannes (St. John?) in *Ordet* and Pastor Tomas (doubting Thomas?) in *Winter Light* position themselves at opposite ends of the Lutheran spectrum. Blasphemous Johannes, a maverick disciple of Kierkegaard, who had controversially attacked the Danish Church, has given himself over to delusions of the Second Coming, wandering through wind-swept dunes and seeming to walk on air, as Jesus had once walked on water, proclaiming himself the living Christ and seeing himself as the creator of divine miracles. Conversely, since the death of his wife, the orthodox Pastor Tomas has never stopped doubting his articles of faith. Märta accuses him of a failure of compassion, of an inability to love and, 'a special indifference to Jesus Christ'. During his writing of the screenplay, Bergman had told Vilgot Sjöman that he envisaged his pastor as a man with 'a hatred of Christ', as envious and jealous as Bergman, a neglected pastor's son, had been during his childhood, when he imagined Jesus as the favoured brother in the eyes of the father (Sjöman 2007 [1963]:25). In the final screen version this is never made explicit in any conversation, but Christ's compassion and the Christian belief in his healing powers are conspicuous by their absence. All traces of him have been eradicated except that of pain in crucifixion, the Nietzschean motif of 'the crucified'. No longer seen as divine, Christ is human only in extreme suffering, in the moment of death. At the end the motif is given its sober reality check. Algot, the churchwarden whose faith is unshakeable, points out that Jesus endured uncompromising pain only during the hours of crucifixion before his death. With a crippling back condition that has no cure, he, Algot, a mere mortal is in constant unrelieved pain. For him the appeal of Christ is one of redemption and salvation, while Tomas doubting both can only identify with Christ's suffering, which he links narcissistically to his own.

Dreyer's miracle ending is literally a stitch-up, a spiritual suture. Even Bordwell has to escape briefly from his brilliant formalist reading of Dreyer to acknowledge something more fundamental about the filmmaker's narration: 'The film's drive towards resolution ... is required to overcome the social problems of faith through a Christian principle of closure: miracle' (Bordwell 1981:146). The schismatic conflicts between landowner Borgen, an orthodox Lutheran, and the ascetic Vital Mission sect of Peter the tailor are forgotten, allowing their respective siblings Anders and Anne to wed each other. After Inger's death, Johannes is shaken from his blasphemy and literally lives up to his name – John, New Testament disciple of the Word. Making the transformation from prophet to disciple - the false 'Saviour' who has come in from the cold – he is then placed to instigate the True Miracle of resurrection. To the untutored secular eye, the miracle could be seen as vindication of his heresy, not its relinquishment, but it matters not. Inger is alive again and the miracle is wrought onscreen, much more compelling in its own way than Spielberg, for example, in his spectacular ending to *Close Encounters of the Third Kind* (1970), where his benign aliens finally land on earth. But it is an ending that Bergman's vision of unsurpassing would not tolerate. In *Winter Light* faith is never abandoned but neither is it transcendental. It remains a demanding journey on the road to nowhere.

Postscript: Birth/No Birthing – *Ordet* and *Brink of Life*

Ordet's birth motif recurs four years later in Bergman's hospital drama *Brink of Life* (1958) directed from a screenplay by writer Ulla Isaksson, and fleeting coincidence binds the two films together. Both films are about the failures of childbirth, and real life presses in on both of them. Dreyer had cast the pregnant Birgitte Federspiel as the pregnant Inger, and then later he recorded sounds of her actual birthing when she went into labour to use in postproduction. Unlike Inger's birth, Federspiel's was successful and Dreyer ironically used recorded sounds of her success to intimate Inger's tribulation and loss. Bergman shot much of his film about miscarriage and stillbirth in a real hospital, Stockholm's Karolinska hospital, while upstairs his sister Margareta was successfully giving birth to a baby daughter (Cowie 1992:171). While Dreyer's film resurrects the maternal body that dies in childbirth, Bergman does the opposite. His pregnant women survive, but both lose the form of life they carry in their womb. Cecilia (Ingrid Thulin) is rushed into the ward bleeding heavily from early miscarriage; the overdue child of Stina (Eva Dahlbeck) is stillborn. Both suffer physically in the process and also suffer loss of life within their bodies. While Cecilia's womb contains a foetus that aborts, Stina's contains the child that dies on 'the brink of life'. Bergman's materialism works through the double distress of pain and loss, and his narrative suspense works classically through juxtaposition, in which, however, there is no happy ending. Cecilia's miscarriage, which begins the film, may be connected to her unhappy marriage; Stina's stillbirth (through forceps delivery), which ends it, occurs to a happily married woman looking forward to parenthood. Stina who begins in the film in high spirits, healthy and expectant and sympathetic to Cecilia's loss, ends it looking like a wraith, a sickbed ghost suffering even greater loss. Dreyer trades off the miracle of life in which Inger's stillborn child is extracted from her womb as a quartered foetus, for the miracle of resurrection, where the dead child is conveniently forgotten as the mother returns to this world. But Bergman offers us no miracle, neither the miracle of life nor of resurrection. The failure of Stina's child to emerge alive from its mother's womb is a cruelty of nature for which there is no consolation, the ultimate act of unsurpassing in the human condition. Dahlbeck, with her frizzy and very artificial blonde wig, may be an ironic lookalike, made up by Bergman to resemble Dreyer's Federspiel, but also to suffer a very different fate where there is no miracle of life, let alone a miracle of transfiguration.

Bergman and Tarkovsky: Apocalypse and Resurrection

In 1972, Tarkovsky, in conversation with Leonid Kozlov, named Bresson's *Diary of a Country Priest* (1951) as his favourite film, but his top ten list included three Bergman films: *Winter Light*, *Wild Strawberries* and *Persona* (Lasica 1993). One film missing from the list was *The Seventh Seal*, understandable since in my view it does not compare with the three that he named. Yet I would argue that it is as indispensable to his first great masterpiece, *Andrei Rublev* (1966), as Eisenstein's epics, *Alexander Nevsky* (1938) and *Ivan the Terrible* (1944–1946). Though Tarkovsky responds to Bergman's tortured evanescent religiosity, in no sense does he see the Swede as a symbolist or metaphysical director. 'I don't understand ... how people can talk about Bergman's "symbolism"', he wrote, 'Far from being symbolic, he seems to me, through an almost biological naturalism, to arrive at the spiritual truth about human life that is important to him' (Tarkovsky 2008:149). Tarkovsky retains the link to naturalism, partly with Bergman's example in front of him, but also he uses it as a launch pad to probe the transcendental. And his moving camera is the prime instrument. It glides forward without seeming effort, or creates its own semicircular rhythms of searching, as if it is an instrument of revelation through motion, a motion that is not human but detached, at times almost godlike. Bergman's camera might move too, to keep up with its subjects in motion; for example, in the parallel tracking that keeps abreast of its running figures in *Persona* or *Shame*. But its prime posture is a still concentration, a frozen focus in which the camera only moves to capture the movement of subjects within the frame. By contrast Tarkovsky's use of the moving camera in *Andrei Rublev*, *Solaris* (1972) and *Mirror* (1975) still remains the most lyrical in all of film history.

Bergman's *The Seventh Seal* and *Rublev* share an imagined medieval setting in their respective countries and both directors take some poetic licence with their history: Bergman compressing the return from the Crusades with the onset of the Black Death, and Tarkovsky compressing his fictional narration of the Princes' Wars and the Mongol–Tatar invasions with Rublev's artisan decoration of new Orthodox churches at Vladimir, Tvenigorod and Moscow. Both films are about journeys. Antonius Block's plague-ridden homecoming is a journey by horseback with his cynical squire Jöns through southern Sweden to his ancestral home. Tarkovsky's Rublev, played by his favourite actor Anatoly Solonitsyn, is an artist-monk who travels with two colleagues, Kirill and Daniil, from the monastery of Andronikov via Moscow to the cathedral at Vladimir, where Rublev and his fellow artisans paint the last judgment. Just as Block is teased and tormented by the figure of Death whom Bergman makes distinctly demonic, Rublev faces the prospect of death when the Mongol–Tatar army, aided by one of the local Muscovite princes, attacks the local population and sacks the cathedral. Having killed one invader with an axe to prevent rape, his general failure to protect the holy site leads him into silence and exile from the world. Only in the final episode, after the miraculous casting of the new bell by a young bell-ringer who has escaped the plague, does Rublev resurrect his art. Boriska, the bell-ringer, in that respect serves the same narrative function as Jof and Mia, the travelling players in Bergman's film. They are untormented survivors of catastrophe, material and visceral in their instincts, yet endowed with grace when disease has consumed those around them. While Block and Rublev both agonize about God and the seeming absence of grace, they are its naïve recipients who give hope in their respective stories to the human race. Yet Bergman's film is one of ultimate darkness while Tarkovsky's is about the resurrection of light. Block's fate is death, preordained in a way that makes Jof and Mia helpless, while Rublev is resurrected by witnessing the triumph of faith over probability in the casting of the bell. *The Seventh Seal* is a parable about the survival of goodness amid apocalyptic ruin, but *Rublev* is about the resurrection of goodness and of faith out of ruin. In the period of the Cold War when the nuclear threat loomed large, Bergman's history film works as a post-mortem on the world of ideals – all ideals. Yet a decade later Tarkovsky's film is the opposite. It is about the emergence of Russian Orthodoxy out of a period of confusion and destruction in early Russia, the long triumphant transplant of Orthodox iconography and belief from Constantinople in the East, where it had been shattered, to an emergent Russian nation in the North where it took on a new lease of life.

Both filmmakers had their distance, of course, from Christian faith and both pursued film careers within secular states that based their rationale on social progress through different economic systems. Both also show little interest in the consumer universe of modernity (Tarkovsky, 2008:42–43). But there is a vital difference. Bergman's neo-protestant individualism and his simultaneous attraction to Nietzsche provided the figure of his aristocratic knight, socially isolated by superior rank as well as assailed by fundamental doubt. But Rublev is an artisan versed in humility, a servant of God who aims to be a servant of his people. For Bergman, after his disastrous early encounter with national socialism, emergent individualism had become by the end of the 1950s the dominant postwar, and bourgeois, predicament; and it was often a predicament of solitude. But Tarkovsky's world view superimposed two forms of communitarianism, one secular and communist, the other closet and Orthodox, neither of them Western European in the social-democratic sense. While Bergman's tormented heroes may seek identification with Christ the crucified, the figure of suffering, Tarkovsky sees the painted Christ icon as a living source of the divine, the coexistence of the sacred and the profane, of immanence and transcendence (Bird 2004:7; Dalle Vache 1996:138). Thus it is that in his moving image, his four basic elements of nature – earth, water, wind and fire – seem imbued in all their material being with iconic aspects of the divine: they are radiant with intimations of the Beyond. The dynamic filming of the four elements translates the still, two-dimensional divinity of the icon back into the filmic three-dimensionality of the probing, searching image, in which the image moves within the frame as the frame itself moves through track and zoom and space and time. Attempts to see in Tarkovsky's camera any 'replication' of the two-dimensional icon are thus mistaken. Tarkovsky's characters are not outsiders to a flat screen seeking a way in to its radiant truth of the divine. The tracking shot and the long take implicate them in the movement towards transcendence and the field of action is recessional, scrolling back to vanishing point. The gamble of Tarkovsky's cinema is to seek out the divine within a three-dimensional space that, unlike Bergman's, is almost always in motion and obliterates the separations of the close-up, the reverse angle and the reaction shot, the filmic tropes of uncertainty and solitude that define Bergman's chamber cinema at its best.

True, Tarkovsky's characters may, as Chris Marker has noted in his brilliant documentary *A Day in the Life of Andrei Arsenevitch* (1999), seek out transcendence through passing over to 'the other side' – behind enemy lines for the young Ivan in wartime, the orbit of Solaris for the space station astronauts in the film of the same name, or the mysterious Zone in *Stalker* (1979). But the other side also corresponds to something within themselves: the other-worldly is also this-worldly. In *Rublev*, Tarkovsky tries to reimagine the world of a medieval Russia under the Tatar yoke where the miracle of resurrection for orthodox Christianity – transplanted from Byzantium – has become possible as part of a national awakening. That is to say, his film world reconstructs the material world that, in his view, had released the Beyond from its inaccessibility and made it part of the world of the living in north-eastern Europe. However, the hazardous journey of Andrei in brutal times does not make of him a Christ figure, a mimetic Jesus substitute in the dangerous early days of Holy Russia. Rather it juxtaposes his fantasy of the Passion enacted during a Russian winter in episode 2 with his subsequent fate, which is an uncertain journey of affirmation and celebration full of brutal setbacks, an iconic resurrection of the divinity of Christ on Rublev's native land. It is enacted through his vision for the adornment of sacred places that communicate the divine through the material textures of paint and plaster and stone. Tarkovsky adopts a special strategy of withholding for the scenario of enactment. In his black and white film he bequeaths a breathtaking colour epilogue where Rublev's extant work in sacred places becomes the source of artistic montage, final evidence of the legacy of a man we scarcely see at work during the course of the film.

We can call this form of ellipsis 'modernist suspense', an anti-melodrama that goes against the Hollywood cliché of the passionate artist at the easel, at its most full-blown in, for example, Minnelli's Van Gogh film, *Lust for Life* (1956). But there is a deeper reason that comes through in episode 4 on 'The Last Judgment', the famous fresco that Rublev painted in the Vladimir cathedral. If Andrei's labours are an integral part in Tarkovsky's vision of the Russian resurrection of the Divine Christ, then the last judgment is an apocalyptic moment of catastrophe that Rublev – and Tarkovsky – are reluctant to instigate. Bergman's *Seventh Seal*, with its Black Death and studied reference to Revelations, is a medieval rendering of that apocalyptic vision, embodied in the title of the film itself. But Tarkovsky is intent on reversing the Bergman motif through the transcending of catastrophe. His motive for withholding images of The Last Judgment until the epilogue is not soviet or humanist, as some critics suggest, but his own specialized instance of the *Bilderverbot*, where images of resurrection must first resonate and images of pain and destruction be surpassed. Tarkovsky of course cues absence in a typically downbeat manner. Andrei is absent, his team bored and idle. Nothing much is happening in the cathedral. We then see Andrei and Daniil discussing the fresco out in the spring countryside, when Andrei claims that he does not want to scare people. The Last Judgment, at this critical point in the fragile history of an emergent Russia, goes against the recuperation of the divine. The 'absence' of the fresco is then offset by something else closer at hand – material catastrophe in the autumn of the same year when the Tatar–Russian alliance brutally desecrates the cathedral in a rite of pagan triumph. This is 'The Raid' of episode 5 that traumatizes Rublev after forcing him into the anti-Christian act of murder; yet by implication provides him with the material for the fresco of the last judgment. In retrospect it poses a tantalizing question. Has he painted the fresco after the sacking of the cathedral (Johnson and Petrie 1994:83)? For its last episode, the film jumps eleven years to a miracle to which Andrei is at first peripheral. The art of artist worship is continued by the bell-ringer's son Boritsky, who has outlived the plague and who finally casts the bell, not through artisan expertise, but through sheer tenacity and an act of faith. The artisan's miracle is thus highly personal and yet totally impersonal at the same time. It makes his name but also works through him. Resurrection and the keeping of the faith work through a labour of love to which many contribute, and which is passed down from generation to generation.

Tarkovsky's elusive modernism runs through the structure of the film. He replaces the continuous chronological and compressed narrative of *The Seventh Seal*, readable at all times, with the narrative episode in *Rublev* that is an enigmatic slice of time, or a slice off time: an episode that is self-sufficient, that forms an epiphany, a happening of such intensity that it is entire unto itself, even though its meaning is never obvious and even though it belongs to a broader genealogy. The seven episodes here, unlike *Mirror*, are chronological and dated onscreen, but since they also elide time there is no clear meaning that can necessarily be read through continuity. We constantly ask ourselves: what has happened in between? The prologue, which does not involve Rublev, and the epilogue, which shows us only glimpses of his finished art, give us no clues. The disconnection of the episodes in time and space may be close to the pattern of the gospels but is more elusive. If Jesus dominates the gospels, Rublev slides in and out of focus, sometimes alone, sometimes part of a monastic trinity, sometimes absent from the frame, sometimes the possible origin of dreams or fantasies, such as the Russian crucifixion in winter, which may or may not be his vision. Rublev in effect, comes and goes. He glides through the picture, whereas Bergman's knight is the picture, the motor of events and the perennial witness of events beyond his control. The contrast is moot: doomed and quixotic noble charisma on the one hand, enduring artisan humility on the other. Bergman uses history to intimate the impending apocalypse of Nordic Christianity, in which the distant past mirrors the crisis of his own time; Tarkovsky uses a distant and buried history to celebrate the birth and survival of Russian Christianity in an epoch of the atheist state.

The Past in the Present/The Past in the Future: *Wild Strawberries* and *Mirror*, *Persona* and *Solaris*

Tarkovsky once criticized *Wild Strawberries* for being a memory film, like *8½*, in which the director's persona, his autobiographical self, hinders the creation of the memory-image. While Fellini's film has clear autobiographical elements, Tarkovsky is wilfully wrong about Bergman's memory film, perhaps because it was such a direct source of inspiration for both *Solaris* and for *Mirror*, which are guided by images that come out of the past and use the key motif of the doubled image of the persona of the female lead that *Wild Strawberries* originates. We can note here that Bibi Andersson, who plays both Sara, the fiancée of Borg's youth and Sara the hitchhiker in Borg's present car journey, was an actress that Tarkovsky seriously considered for the lead roles in *Solaris* (taken by Natalia Bondarchuk) and then *Mirror* (taken by Margarita Terekhova)(Tarkovsky 1991:77). This doubling of past and present filtered through the figure of Sara was a crucial template for Tarkovsky's vision, which works in a very different way to *Wild Strawberries* and takes the doubling time-image into new dimensions. But let us say first why Bergman's film is not autobiographical. For a start, Isak Borg (played by Victor Sjöström at the end of his acting career), is a figure from a previous generation, a science doctor who, in terms of dates, could have been Bergman's father, not a facsimile of self. His memories are not historically memories of Bergman's childhood but Bergman's imagination of a previous generation. It is true that Borg's character may combine, as Bergman has suggested, elements of his father and himself but if anything the nearest figure to Bergman would be Borg's son Evald (played by Gunnar Björnstrand), whose marriage to Marianne (Ingrid Thulin) is in trouble. Moreover, the marital reunion in Lund of the troubled couple after Borg and Marianne's trip from Stockholm remains one of the less convincing sequences in the film. This is a great Bergman memory film because it is not about Bergman's memories and in a way is not about actual memory at all. It is rather about virtual memory, the imagining of things past, when the subject was not present and yet when his absence was critical to the future course of his life. The past is haunted not by memory itself but by virtual memories, in which the subject places himself where he was never positioned at the time.

Bergman breaks with his earlier use of flashback conventions because Borg does not flash back to his family past, but rather walks into it as he breaks his car journey and observes events from his youth that he did not witness. Thus he is both present and absent – an observer from the future of events that happened at the time of his absence and hauntingly 'behind his back'. Thus Isak, as an old man, 'observes' in his mind's eye what he did not actually see as a young man, but the medium of film turns the act of imaginary observing into a moving image. The 'walk-back' supplants the flashback and in turn becomes an inspiration for Theo Angelopoulos in his end-of-the-century films of remembrance, *Eternity and a Day* (1998) and *Ulysses Gaze* (1995). Yet at the end, after Isak has received his honorary doctorate, Bergman adds to the walk-back the Borg dream in Lund that returns to the scene of the memory and scrambles it through guilt and association with other failures of Borg's life. And it completes too the cycle of the day and the film itself, which had started just before waking in Stockholm with Borg's dream of his own death.

The film thus starts with an old man's nightmare of impending death and ends with a nightmare whose aftermath is a simple sort of redemption. The three hitchhikers, led by Sara, turn up outside the house to serenade the professor before their onward trip to Italy. As the two boys fade into the night, Sara returns to tell him it is Isak she loves 'today, tomorrow and every day'. Thus Sara's contemporary double atones for the original Sara's primal desertion in the simplest of ways. This is earthly redemption, so fleeting it might go unnoticed, but the surprise of the serenade after the darkness of the dream shows Bergman at the height of his dramatic powers, turning nightmare into healing, giving us the most touching of touching moments. Spiritual healing is material, not transcendental, present in the body of the world as the simplest of gestures. A day in the life of the ageing Isak Borg thus becomes, through Bergman's memory-inversion, a life in the day of the eminent professor. Time is squeezed like a lemon in its taut duration, but in doing so it also balloons outwards to immense proportions. Bergman's film universe contracts in order to expand – and how!

Let us consider its relationship to *Mirror*. Tarkovsky's film follows more tightly the pattern of his own lifetime, from early childhood to impending middle age. In

Mirror there is briefly the appearance of a figure based autobiographically on Tarkovsky's real father as the wartime soldier and estranged husband (Oleg Iankovsky), who appears unexpectedly on leave to visit his children. Meanwhile the poems overlaying the narrative at crucial moments are his real father's poems – the poems of Arseni Tarkovsky read in Arseni's voice. The offscreen voice reinforces the mystery of the absent figure: the real voice of Tarkovsky's father shadows the figure of the fictional father. And the aural offscreen is mirrored later in the 1970s figure of the adult Alexei, who like his father is heard but not seen: this time present in the same apartment, in conversation with his wife or son but always out of frame, invisible. Just as Bergman had delivered a coup de grâce in the doubling of Bibi Andersson as Sara, so it is that in the doubling of the mother, Tarkovsky delivers his coup de grâce – the double-image of Margarita Terekhova playing both mother (Maria) and wife (Natalia) in Tarkovsky's autobio-fiction. She is both the waiting wife (of Arseni) and mother (of Andrei/Alexei) in the 1930s, and the troubled wife (of Alexei) and mother (of Andrei junior/Ignat) in the 1970s. Her cardigan and long skirt in the 1930s at the summertime dacha are replaced by the brown leather jacket and corduroy jeans of the 1970s in the Moscow apartment in winter. To intensify the effect of this mirror of generations, there is similar doubling in the casting of Ignat Daniltsev as twelve-year-old Alexei in wartime and as the twelve-year-old Ignat, Alexei's son, in the 1970s. The mirrors of persona are also mirrors of history, the reflecting prisms of generations in which visual and genetic likeness are combined. Just as Sara/Bibi Andersson is a young woman of different generations torn between two suitors, so Maria/Margarita Terekhova is the figure of a married woman and young mother of different generations whose marriage is falling apart.

Here the strategies of Bergman and Tarkovsky diverge. The figure of Sara in time past is filtered purely through Borg's dreams and memories: but through whose memory is the figure of Maria sitting on the gate at the dacha filtered? It could be Maria herself, yet Tarkovsky eschews the purely subjective. His images of the past are highly personal yet also impersonal: they are his childhood memories, his mother's memories of the same time and a filmic reconstruction in which Tarkovsky rebuilds the old dacha that has been destroyed, purely for the staging of his film. Yet Tarkovsky also uses recorded documentary footage of the politics of the period to juxtapose against personal film linking two generations of his family. He uses images of civilians in Barcelona fleeing air raids in the Spanish Civil War, images (found in the archives) of Soviet troops wading arduously through Lake Siwash in Crimea as they begin a tentative advance – and sudden ambush – against retreating Germans, and later images of the 1945 liberation in Prague and Berlin and the atomic explosion at Hiroshima, followed by contemporary images of conflict between Soviet soldiers and Red Guard militants on the border with China. More crucially the director used as models for his staging, photographic images of his family at the Ignatievo dacha of Pavel Gorchakov, where he had stayed during three summers from 1935 to 1937, resourced from the many photographs shot by his godfather Lev Gorning who was a close family friend and had sold the negatives to Mosfilm (Synessios 2001:42–44). Thus Tarkovsky's reconstruction is not only effected through personal dreams and family memory, but also through photography: the objective register that complements the subjective impression of the past. Gorning's photographs made possible not only Tarkovsky's exact reconstruction of the villa for filming purposes but also for clothing, design and fixtures. They were the vital springboard for reconstruction, but also a photographic register of the personal, which is complemented by the documentary register of the political that Tarkovsky takes from the film archives. Interestingly, and clearly to satisfy the authorities, Tarkovsky in his final edit uses documentary in chronological order, whereas the autobio-fiction is circular, starting off in early childhood and ending with his mother and father outside the dacha during an earlier summer contemplating his possible birth.

Here we can chart the difference with Bergman. Isak Borg's journey from Stockholm to Lund is a journey in the present that absorbs the past, as it figures in the professor's present dreams and imagination – an isolate's journey of atonement for his failures, his losses, his coldness towards others. *Mirror* is a memory journey into the past which is familial and collective, a journey that celebrates endurance and the sensuous nature of a collective life lived amid beauty and adversity. Both films have a special bearing on the view of cinema as poetry. Like *Vertigo* (1958), *Wild Strawberries* signifies the emergence of a cinema of poetry that Pasolini has analysed, where the disturbed mind of a bourgeois subject that is not a disguised portrait of the director but a discrete imaginary being, allows a new freedom of exploration in the moving image, a focus on pure form that turns cinema into narrative poetry. These films of Bergman and Hitchcock still remain plot-driven as opposed to later more developed versions of cinematic poetry, à la Pasolini, such as Antonioni's *Red Desert* or Bergman's *Persona* and *Hour of the Wolf*. We could say that Tarkovsky's cine-poetry offers an Eastern alternative to this

European modernism. His poetry of cinematic form works through the individual and the collective at the same time, collective remembrance in *Mirror*, collective resurrecting of the divine in *Andrei Rublev*, collective experience of outer space in *Solaris*. Instead of the discrete, inwardly disturbed bourgeois subject of Pasolini (and Bergman), we have the externally disturbed collective subject of Tarkovsky mediated by a central figure who is not, however, divorced from others but lives with and through them.

Wild Strawberries is guided by Borg's voiceover, cueing in moments of remembrance, virtual recollections and disturbed dreams. Yet Tarkovsky dispenses with a central and mediating voice. Three dream sequences in *Mirror* can be separated out and enumerated in plot synopsis, as Synessios does (ibid.:6–9), but all can be challenged as has been done by other critics. The ontological status of the sequences is never fully clear, nor is the identity of the dreamer. In Bergman the dreams are Borg's dreams signified by first-person voiceover, or by waking fear: there is a rudimentary pattern.

And yet the dreams which occur towards the end of Borg's car journey augment the walk-backs, the virtual recollections which mark their inception; they also echo the nightmare of death that had started the film as Borg wakes at dawn. Bergman's patterns and variations are just as complex as Tarkovsky's even if they are less enigmatic. And both films end with the pre-life of the central subject. Borg comforts himself with bucolic images of his distant mother and father who wave back when he calls silently, while Tarkovsky ends *Mirror* with a sustained bucolic image of Alexei's mother and father discussing conception. Both could be read as idealized images of the origin of self in the mutual love of one's progenitors, virtual memories by the adult subject who could never have been there. The difference in chronotope is also vital. Borg projects the past as wishful reverie, as virtual memory. Yet in Tarkovsky, the absent Alexei is only there to narrate sporadically and usually fails to tell us much at all, since many of the images of memory are ones that Alexei as a very young child could not have had (Johnson and Petrie 1994:116–17). Tarkovsky's images of time past work only as collective images. They are there to be judged without guidance and pieced together by an alert spectator. Since we have no image of the adult Alexei, who has been consistently offscreen throughout, we cannot directly flash back or walk back though his eyes. We must make the leap of cinematic imagination for ourselves, and plunge into the spiral of Tarkovsky's enigma. And yet for spectators to share that diffuse, collective memory is the moment of transcendence. When Tarkovsky's film world works its wondrous alchemy on his life-world, the spectator completes it, consummates it and shares the moment. The question of whose memory it is recedes. It is the shared memory of those who were never there. It is ours.

If *Mirror* gives us a life transcended – surpassed through the magic of a universal memory that is everywhere and nowhere; *Solaris*, three years earlier, had been a study in transfiguration, and one that more completely fused *Wild Strawberries* with *Persona* in a genre that Bergman never had any inclination of using – science fiction. Yet *Solaris*, adapted from the popular novel of Polish writer Stanislaw Lem, is not so much science fiction as deconstruction of science fiction, so much so that Lem, who had intensive discussions with Tarkovsky, viewed the finished film with intense dislike. Lem, like many science-fiction writers, was an optimist who believed the progressive promise of new technologies, their power to overcome the dangers and limits of the human condition. Tarkovsky's film of his book is faithful to detail, yet does anything but. It is science fiction that upends science fiction and a study in transfiguration in which the central figures remain the same. While *Andrei Rublev* transcends through its artisan restaging of the Orthodox second coming of a Byzantine Christ, and *Mirror* through a poetry of memory that surpasses surrounding catastrophe, *Solaris* points up the Tarkovsky paradox of earthly transcendence in the sharpest way of all. All is transfigured through the return of the same. The arc of the *Solaris* narrative is at once awesome and ineffable. We surpass the earth through the act of transcendence yet in the end the act of transcendence brings us down to earth once more.

It is the only true romantic film that Tarkovsky ever made, yet at the same time the most enigmatic of his modernist innovations. Poetic, elliptical, uncompromising, *Mirror* has its anchor in identifiable history but here, apart from the opening sequence, there is little context. The sensibility is Russian, the names are not. 'Solaris' is no closer to Moscow than it is to New York. Psychoanalysis, atomic physics and neuroscience, Don Quixote, Breughel and Leonardo: the references are polyphonic. We could say the opening sequences by the lake and in the lakeside dacha signal to us in a familiar Tarkovsky landscape. But where is this house on the emerald fringe of an astonishing landscape, other than somewhere on earth? Tarkovsky makes the point in his elliptical cut to the next major sequence, a fixed car shot at speed. It was filmed ingeniously, on a new superhighway into Tokyo to confuse easy identification – the countryside Russian and verdantly green, the black and white metropolis distinctly un-Soviet. And yet Tarkovsky's scintillating emerald earth is Russian, the dacha the Russian 'home', the rooted point of nature outside a modernity that is global and looks outward to the cosmos. The drama of the Russian home here replays itself in space and the chamber drama of the modest country home – the Bergman trope, of course, is the solitary coastal cottage – becomes a space chamber drama within the astronauts' space station, with psychologist Kris Kelvin (Donatas Banionis) and his two colleagues orbiting the sentient ocean of Solaris. And yet though it is outer-space chamber drama with its semicircular corridors exuding the gloss of futuristic design, it is still intimate chamber drama with its subjects becalmed and confronted by their frailties.

Bergman's metaphorical inner space that marks *Persona*, where identity is explored within confined spaces on the edge of vastness that is the Baltic, is transformed here into the confined spaces of the oval spacecraft on the edge of vastness that is the Solaris Ocean. One identity transfer, in which the mute Elisabet appropriates and devours the persona of the uncertain Alma, is replaced by another form of doubling. Responding to the rogue radiation attacks from the spacecraft, Solaris appropriates the desires and memories of its astronaut attackers and sends them back in proto-human form. Kelvin's dead lover (or is it wife?), the young and beautiful Hari (Natalia Bondarchuk), returns as simulacrum, as identical copy made flesh.

Here Tarkovsky reverses transcendence, in which conventionally the earthly becomes ethereal or heavenly. 'Hari', as a copy of the departed lover is both a ghostly product of planet Solaris, yet a 'copy' that seeks out the materiality of planet Earth and refuge from the nightmare of mechanical reproduction through transfiguration into the one unique being, a person of the flesh in love with another person of the flesh. While Bergman's films have always echoed the impossibility of being heavenly, *Solaris* turns the striving on its head. It is about the impossible striving to be accepted as human – reverse resurrection. Tarkovsky uses the metaphysics of science fiction to reaffirm his faith in the materiality of the grounded world – the Tarkovsky paradox. The girl from Solaris wishes to inhabit planet Earth but will never do so. The space crew, lead by Sartorius, claim that if she dies other identical duplicates can replace her and yet, in her call for conscience, she is much more human than the scientists. The nature of transfiguration thus changes too. While *Persona* climaxes in the displacement of Alma's face by that of Elisabet Vogler's, despite the nurse's resistance, the face of Hari always looks the same as Tarkovsky explores a transfiguration of the soul that cannot take place. Bondarchuk can thus play any number of Hari substitutes without changing her face, her hair, or her clothes. Yet there is an echo of *Persona* too. In the role of a substitute who wishes not to be one, Bondarchuk rejects the role of Hari and kills herself with liquid oxygen to 'free' Kelvin from his dilemma. 'No, I am not Hari!' she utters in despair, echoing the words of Bibi Andersson as Sister Alma. 'No, I am not Elisabet Vogler!' as she is about to be swallowed up in the persona of the other woman.

The film series *Vampyr–Persona–Solaris* presents us with the rise, fall and rise of the transcendental. *Vampyr* blends four-dimensional space with the twilight world of the undead. Bergman humanizes vampirism and *Persona* denies its transcendental value. Vogler is a role-playing actress devouring the personae of others in order to fill her empty heart and further her profession. *Solaris* resurrects Hari from the dead in outer space where she is the anti-vampire, the externalized emanation of Eros and conscience that her doomed figure blends with an instinctual sense of her own mortality, even though she is not strictly mortal. But if the planet can resurrect a version of the 'human' in outer space it cannot guarantee its journey back down to Earth. Solaris merely externalizes the being of the suicidal lover that the haunted Kelvin had once deserted. And like *Vertigo* where Scottie precipitates the death of Madeleine the second time around, Kelvin is doomed to repeat his earthly trauma.

We can now see, finally, how the blending of *Wild Strawberries* and *Persona* was a launch pad for the greatest feat of Tarkovsky's cinematic imagination. Just as Isak Borg is haunted by guilt about the woman he let slip from his grasp, so is Kelvin. And like Borg, Kelvin too is 'guilty of guilt'. The Solaris Ocean throws back at him the human figment of his guilty imagination in the form of the woman he had rejected. But while the modern Sara in Borg's journey is very different in demeanour from the distant Sara of Borg's youth, in *Solaris* the figure of Hari, complete with her dress of autumnal colours, the brown and ochre of the autumnal earth, is the identical copy, who can be duplicated to infinity, the return of the same without variation. While Borg reconciles himself to the past, at the end of his film Tarkovsky's *Solaris* inherits the enigma of *Persona*. How two women go their separate ways at the end of the film goes against the grain of the vampiric act that precedes it. Bergman cuts elliptically and without obvious explanation. Likewise Tarkovsky undercuts the meaning of Kelvin's homecoming in the very last sequence of the picture. Returning to the dacha to greet his father, Kris adopts the submissive posture of Leonardo's prodigal son. The staging of the long shot starts at ground level, then turns into an ascending crane shot, which some have seen as a Tarkovsky God-shot, where father and son are viewed from on high. Tarkovsky ups the ascent with an abrupt cut from crane shot to plane shot, that pulls back ever upwards until his subjects are tiny dots beneath. A return-of-patriarchy reading would have left it there: God, Father, Son. But then Tarkovsky makes his final telling cut, disguised by cloud formation to a point at which the dacha is on a tiny island on the earth's surface, just like the tiny islands that are beginning to form on the Solaris Ocean. Is the return of the prodigal son then no more than a materialization of a mental image from the planet's ocean, and Kelvin's return imagined rather than actual? Tarkovsky's abrupt and unexpected cut gives a reverse meaning, all the while providing the technical continuity of retraction. Is Kelvin still on the space station, hallucinating his return to Earth, just as he had hallucinated the return of Hari? Tarkovsky's single cut upends his whole film, just as Bergman's cut from Alma's close-up dissolution of self to her long shot leaving, compos mentis, suitcase in hand, leaves a wound that cannot be sutured. Both deal in the subtlest form of suspense. Is planet Solaris starting to suck the life out of planet Earth, just as Elisabet Vogler had sucked the life out of Sister Alma? The ending of each film is open, yet poised on the proverbial knife-edge. And you don't even need digital replay. The images from both films are strong enough to replay in the imagination and to haunt the spectator who gets involved with them.

CHAPTER THREE

Lure of the Archipelago
Bergman–Godard–New Wave

Some critics contend that Bergman's modernism 'followed' Jean-Luc Godard and the French New Wave (Dixon 2000:44–61). The truth is the opposite. It was the fascination the *Cahiers du cinéma* group felt for 1950s Bergman that acted as a trigger for their New Wave innovations in the 1960s. Delayed French release dates prevented instant response to Bergman, but from 1956 to 1959 the following films all made the *Cahiers* top ten annual list – *Summer Interlude, Sawdust and Tinsel, Smiles of a Summer Night, Dreams* and *Wild Strawberries*. The momentum continued into the 1960s with *Through a Glass Darkly, The Silence, All these Women* (1964) and *Hour of the Wolf* all becoming critical favourites, *Winter Light* making it to number three on the list in 1965, and the coup de grâce, *Persona*, at number one in 1967. In 1958, on the occasion of a Cinémathèque retrospective, Jean-Luc Godard had led a big *Cahiers* tribute in his short piece 'Bergmanorama', where he called the Swedish director, 'the last great romantic' and 'the most original auteur in modern European cinema' (Milne 1986:75–80). Eric Rohmer wrote at length about *Dreams*, Jacques Rivette reviewed *Summer Interlude*, and in his debut feature *The Four Hundred Blows* (1959), François Truffaut paid tribute to *Summer with Monika* with a celebrated Harriet Andersson poster in the foyer of a cinema visited by the young Antoine Doinel. For all of them, Bergman was an observer of the contemporary world whose fresh vision struck an immediate chord.

Homage continued into the 1960s. In 1966, in a brief section of *Masculine-Feminine*, Godard filmed a fragment of a spoof Bergman film starring Birger Malmsten and vaguely resembling *The Silence*, which had also inspired his earlier 1964 film *A Married Woman*. Then, in 1968, both he and Jean-Louis Comolli hailed the reflexive boldness of *Persona* and *Hour of the Wolf* as new advances in contemporary cinema, where the film itself assumed a momentum far above and beyond the input of its auteur. Going in the opposite direction, we could say Claude Chabrol's *Les Biches* (1968) ingeniously turned the doubling, lesbian motifs of *Persona* back into murder and melodrama in the style of Hitchcock. Godard meanwhile made use of Bibi Andersson's sexually explicit 'beach confession' to Liv Ullmann in *Persona* as a template for Mireille Darc's sexually explicit confession to her analyst at the start of *Weekend* (1967): a confession liberally peppered with long sections taken from Bataille's *The Story of the Eye*. Bergmanesque intimate revelation thus turns into Godardian cine-literary quotation. In the critical realm, with a new Marxist editorial team in place after 1968, *Cahiers* ignored Bergman's work completely, the journal only making amends in 1980 with Alain Bergala's positive review of *From the Life of the Marionettes* (Bergala 1980), a film that also received accolades from the most talented of the new generation of French critics: Serge Daney. Among post–New Wave directors, Philippe Garrel, Jacques Doillon and Olivier Assayas have all acknowledged the enduring impact of Bergman upon their own work (www.bergmanorama.webs.com). And Garrel's later intimate chamber films such as *J'entends plus la guitare* (1991) and *Sauvage innocence* (2001) seem at times a pure reworking of Bergman in the age of heroin.

If we go back to Bergman's work in the 1950s we find its double significance for the course of European cinema. It was not just a springboard for his later modernism, it was also a trigger for the modernisms of the Nouvelle Vague – Nordic modernism, we might say, versus Parisian modernisms, but both with a common root. Here was a director making daring films about a 1950s generation in Europe to which they could look up, while casting aspersions on the French 'cinema of quality' they despised. Not only that, but Bergman was a key bridge between Europe and Hollywood. For *Cahiers* critics, *A Lesson in Love* possessed the comic brio of Lubitsch and Hawks, while *Summer Interlude* and *Waiting Women* possessed the flashback bravado of Welles or Mankiewicz. In European terms, the location shoot of the archipelago films rivalled the assurance and atmospherics of the Italian neo-realists. Here Bergman provided a model for two key things: firstly the boldness and fluidity of the island location where narrative went beyond the strictures of dramatic tension to assume its own rhythms, and secondly the transformation of Hollywood romance into a new ontology of passion that freed itself from the strictures of melodrama, an existential cinema of enchantment and disillusion.

Romantics and Moderns: Godard, Rivette and *Summer Interlude*

Let us start then with the seminal impact of *Summer Interlude*. In the 1958 *Cahiers* retrospective, Rivette gave a bold modernist reading of the film (Rivette 1958:45– 47) while Godard made it the centrepiece of his general tribute to Bergman. What did they see in it? For Rivette this film, co-scripted with Herbert Grevenius and shot on the archipelago island of Smådalarö, places Bergman not as Godard's 'last great romantic' but as embryonic modernist, a director who interrogated the very nature of his characters, who focused on states of emotional being rather than on action and who was closer to Strindberg's *The Ghost Sonata* and to Beckett than to Ibsen or early Strindberg (ibid.:45–46). Bergman is not a craftsman, a technical perfectionist: he is a visionary. His films go with the flow and his scenes go beyond the point of dramatic tension to linger and create their own sense of being, even if this comprises distraction and conversational nonsense. And as Bergman interrogates his characters, taking nothing about them for granted, so, in an act of filmic autocritique, he interrogates a previous film he has made in a succeeding one – *Prison* (1949) in *Summer Interlude* and *Summer Interlude* in *The Seventh Seal*. Bergman's development is defined, in effect, by cinematic self-consciousness, a tendency the New Wave took to even greater levels.

Yet Rivette here makes an even more challenging intervention. He sees Bergman's 'metaphysical beauty' as ontological – a cinema of the body – in which the director creates his most memorable effects in the conflict between the density of being and the artifice of the figures out of which it is composed. Bergman's is a tactile cinema, a cinema of the flesh that rejects pure spirituality and brings the spectator up close and personal to the textures of the skin, of water, of sweat and tears (ibid.: 46). The metaphysical mysteries that anglophone audiences searched for in *The Seventh Seal*, *The Virgin Spring* (1960) or *Through a Glass Darkly* were of little interest to Rivette at all. Instead he admired the rawness of emotional being that Bergman's films displayed – above all humiliation, desire, bitterness, regret and on the rebound, pride and lucidity. As well as being a cinema of free expression, which in *Summer Interlude* valued summer light and water, interlude and distraction, the carnal and the luminous, Bergman's cinema is a celebration of the density of being, of the joys (and heartbreaks) of a material world. We could also add that Bergman's vision of play and display in the early films, the stage performances of ballet (*Summer Interlude*), music (*To Joy*) and circus (*Sawdust and Tinsel*), plus the ethos of the travelling players in *The Seventh Seal* and *The Face*, have all fed into the ontological playfulness of Rivette's own cinema, his predilection both for theatrical play in everyday life (*Céline and Julie go Boating* [1974]) and the ontological framing of theatrical rehearsal (*Paris Belongs to Us* [1961], *L'amour fou* [1969], *Gang of Four* [1988]) in which Rivette probes the dialectic between density of being and the artifice of appearance that he first identified in Bergman in 1958.

How, then, did the same film look to Godard? For Godard, the key axis of change is not so much classical to modern as romantic to modern – the romanticism which Godard's 1960s cinema tries to exorcize but never really does. The transition was never, as Godard realized, a clean break. The romantic often proved a shaky foundation for the modernistic edifice. In that respect, Godard's core aesthetic in the pictures up to 1967 was to create a cinema of risk, to dare to build on those shaky foundations. For that reason it is a deliberate aesthetic of the incomplete picture, the half-finished project, the quasi-film starting out afresh by paying homage to its predecessors; and here Godard turned cinematic quotation into a fine art. Godard's onscreen tribute to *Summer Interlude* first came in *Breathless* (1960) where, as Rosenbaum has pointed out (Rosenbaum 1995:20), Seberg's Patricia is given the words of Maj-Britt Nilsson's Marie ten years earlier: 'I'm trying to shut my eyes very tightly so that everything becomes dark. But I can't. It's never completely dark.' Five years later, Godard takes Marie's island journey back into the romantic past as a key source for the fractured pathos that expresses itself most clearly in his rather different 'journey' narrative, *Pierrot le fou*. Godard had claimed that *Summer Interlude* was 'the most beautiful of films' (Milne 1986:76) and many Godard critics would see *Pierrot* with the superb colour photography of Raoul Coutard as the most beautiful of his films. Both evoke with bold masterstrokes what Godard agreed with his interviewer was 'the poetic presence of the sea' (Comolli et al. 1965). *Pierrot* was one of Godard's few films – along with *Le Mépris* (1963) which is partly set in Capri – that features shore and sea and coastline and a film in which he called his feuding lovers 'the last romantic couple', echoing his 1958 description of Bergman as the last romantic director. Before we look at this cult box-office success, which paired his two best actors, Anna Karina (Marianne) and Jean-Paul Belmondo (Ferdinand), we can hone in more closely on Godard's idealization of Bergman as a lone romantic artist and Bergman's sardonic response to it ten years later. In 'Bergmanorama', Godard had proffered a romantic lone-auteur version of Bergman's films as not simply craft but an art form: 'One is always alone; on the set as before the blank page. And for Bergman, to be alone means to ask questions. And to make films means to answer them. Nothing could be more classically romantic' (ibid.). Presented with this quote in 1968 by Stig Björkman, Bergman replied: 'I find Godard's way of putting things bewitching. It's precisely what he does himself, what he has fallen victim to! He's writing about himself' (Björkman et al. 1973:60).Bergman then repeats what he has said many times, that film is a collective praxis in which everyone has to pull together. 'I've felt lonely in the outside world', he goes on 'and for that reason I've taken refuge in a community of feeling, however illusory' (ibid.:62). He could have added of course that he was always in charge, but the statement is still a timely reminder, a stark reversal of much cod history in film modernism. Bergman has been seen for too long as a peripheral loner, an ultra-sensitive auteur, whereas Godard has been celebrated for his didactic celebration of the collective. Yet disintegration of romantic sensibility meant more to Godard than it did to Bergman, and Godard has often been more of a loner in the making of his films than Bergman. Still they do have a distant likeness. Godard was an exception to the French Catholic New Wave – he came from a family of Swiss Protestants. His cinema, like Bergman's, has often worked as an artistic register of the cultural afterlife of European Protestantism, but more obliquely and in ways perhaps that critics have yet to confront. And one other traditional Protestant tendency stands out, uniting both of them – their fanatical work ethic and prodigious output, a compulsion to film without parallel in modern European cinema.

If Bergman's Marie was a prototype for the Godardian woman, then Harriet Andersson's Monika made an even stronger impact on the young French director. It is Godard's fusion of elements from *Summer Interlude* and *Summer with Monika* that paves the way for *Pierrot le fou*. From the former he took the intensity of the landscaped romance, delivered so beautifully by Gunnar Fischer's photography, and transformed it into blazing widescreen colour through the lenses of Raoul Coutard. From the latter film he took something else – the coexistence of love and hate in heterosexual intimacy, as the teenage Monika and Harry, her boyfriend, love and quarrel with little compromise. Godard claimed *Summer Interlude* was actually an autumn film of romantic reverie, comparable to Rousseau's *Confessions*; and *Summer with Monika* a seasonal prequel, a summer film with 'a sordid pessimism reminiscent of *La Nausée*' (Milne 1986:84). *Monika* mixes pleasure and squalor, joy with boredom in equal measure. This constant oscillation marks the key departure from *Summer Interlude*. The latter had its dramatic contrasts in the passage of time between summer and autumn and the ten years between the teenage and the adult Marie, beautifully rendered by Bergman's fluid use of flashback. What it did not have was *Monika*'s sudden alternation of mood and feeling within the flow of time itself. Thus *Pierrot le fou* fuses the visual epiphanies of *Summer Interlude* with the emotional oscillation of *Monika*, Marie's idealism with Monika's opportunism, the rapture of true love with the nausea of disenchantment. As Godard's beautiful couple finally reach the sea, opposites begin to bleed into one another. At the end of their stay on the island they love and hate in equal measure.

There is then, to repeat, more continuity between Bergman's island romanticism and Godard's early modernism than between 1950s and 1960s Bergman. Bergman made the leap from his romantic, panoramic films of the 1950s to his enclosed modernist films of the 1960s – from *Summer Interlude* to *The Silence* and *Persona* – with acrobatic daring, a triumphant leap into the unknown, a journey into dream and abstraction that is breathtaking in its execution. Yet it is also a transition out of natural beauty into poetic nightmare: the break with romanticism is absolute. Godard, who was not part of Bergman's generation, differs: until 1968 he brings those lyric tropes of romance that he finds in Ray, Rossellini, film noir, Bergman and Hitchcock with him into unchartered waters, and he never abandons them. It is Bergman who changed more completely. The core relationship in his Baltic trilogy that ends the 1960s is the stark, unflinching examination of the Ullmann/Von Sydow intimacy-in-trouble; triangular variations on psychic implosion. Before that, in *The Silence* and *Persona* troubled and turbulent intimacy takes place between warring women, as it will again in *Cries and Whispers* and *Autumn Sonata*. By contrast, early Godard brings romance and its discontents forward into modernist idiom with the adventure of the young romantic couple that marks *Breathless* and *Pierrot le fou*, and more austerely through the intimacy triangle of *A Married Woman*. Yet of these three early masterpieces, *Pierrot le fou* is the most defining feature. So what is the key difference between 1950s Bergman and 1960s Godard in their take on the 'end of romance'?

In *Summer Interlude* Bergman films the tragedy of Henrik's diving accident as a sudden, shocking event, a disaster that comes out of the blue. The awkward student breaks his back on concealed rocks by riskily diving into shallow water. There is stilted exaggeration in the staging and yet the impact on the teenage Marie and the death scene in hospital afterwards are shot with genuine power. This is the end of first love, the island romance cut short, taken away in a moment of recklessness. Marie is traumatized in adult life when ten years later she has a true dancer's talent and rational power to function but hides her continuing trauma behind the mask of performer's makeup: 'a painted puppet on a string' she calls herself, no longer blessed with the energy to love. Yet in the run-up to the fatal accident, Bergman had subtly changed the mood of the film. A sense of fatality clouds the air. As autumn approaches and the island idyll draws to a close, Bergman foregrounds in a beautiful floor shot the pirouetting legs of Marie, the rehearsing ballerina, as the sitting Henrik with his pet dog watches intently in the background. His look is tinged with regret and jealousy; her autumn life back in the city is already taking over. Later outside they twice hear the unnerving hoot of an owl as the wind rises and the sky darkens. The subtle shadings of exterior light usher, in true romantic style, organic portents of the danger to come. The film of course had hinted earlier at this loss to come in time present, during the adult Marie's return to the island in late autumn: in the black figure of the shawl-covered Aunt, a figure of death she sees treading a lonely path in the whistling wind and then in the bleak return to the abandoned cottage where she had slept that summer, a room restored by flashback into the site of an island idyll. The return is a moment of foreboding, for us setting the mood for what will later happen in the film, for her returning to what has already happened in her life.

Godard's debt in *Pierrot le fou* to Bergman's film shows in the second act of his three-act picture which, adapted from the fiction of Lionel White, starts and ends as homage to American film noir – here with the topical theme of illicit arms dealing after the end of the Algerian war. Godard's 'summer interlude' when his couple reach the Côte d'Azur and go out to a small island, is also a narrative interlude, an idyllic moment trapped between two phases of a genre film founded on money, murder and betrayal. The noir couple have been rampant – the husband is dead, the money not found, the flight under way (though Godard confounds all three motifs with his enigma variations). But as the film segues into pastoral romance, the 'plot' will soon catch up with them. Another link to Bergman surfaces – Ferdinand's island diary, used and seen here as if it filled in the absent words of Henrik's missing notebook, which kick-started the memories of *Summer Interlude*. We might have expected Marie's sudden recovery of Henrik's notebook twelve years later to trigger his words and memories. In the first flashback sequence it does. But we do not see the pages of the notebook: instead the next sequence at the beach cottage triggers Marie's voiceover: her words and memories. Post-Bergman, Godard switches back again. Brief shots of Ferdinand's diary cue male voiceover, the words and observations of a male lover bemused by the febrile Marianne. For Marianne is an elusive object, a modernistic femme fatale quickly bored by island romance.

What Marianne takes over from Marie is not so much romance as pure movement, a kinetic purity of the moving image. Just as Marie moves impulsively and lyrically through woods and over rocks and sand, like the dancer that she is, so Marianne is a character who takes the lyricism of the Hollywood musical out of its carapace into the settings of everyday life (as Jacques Demy was also doing in *The Umbrellas of Cherbourg* [1964]). Yet her mischievous nature is closer to Bergman's Monika, giving us a triple formula. Marie moves and Henrik clumsily follows, just as Monika moves and Harry (Lars Ekborg) clumsily follows, witness to the one-sided dance scene before their boat is set on fire. In *Pierrot le fou* Marianne moves and Ferdinand elegantly follows, but unlike Bergman's heroes, Ferdinand is his lover's match in every way. All three films are thus existential musicals, whose movements are diversionary trails in loose narration – with Bergman offering us early versions of the Deleuzian 'balade'. In *Summer Interlude* Henrik's gauche, clumsy movements are knowingly contrasted with the smart cynical talk of the Stockholm reporter who a decade later gatecrashes Marie's ballet rehearsal, a razor-sharp Lothario chasing the adult dancer in time present. The movement of Belmondo, however, is full of grace, showing up the onscreen difference between Bergman's male foils – his 'coat-hangers' as he called them – and the male icon of *Breathless*. Belmondo is a prime mover: voice, gesture, movement define him as one of the true stars of European cinema.

We thus find alternate exit routes from the melodrama conundrum that haunted classical Hollywood. In Marie's flashback and voiceover first love is gradually fused with the organic unities of landscape, sea and summer: romance without melodrama, a pure aesthetic of beauty bookended by the trauma of loss. Godard's fugitive lovers initially merge with island, sea and summer in blazing colour, but disenchantment severs the connection. Romance dies as soon as it is born. Ferdinand's words and books drown out Marianne's music and emotions. As Marianne deviously plots, and double-cross follows; bars, tourists, boats and bustle intervene. Culture obliterates nature and, as in *Breathless*, the irresistible plot of film noir that had sparked *l'amour fou* in the first place, catches up with Godard's troubled couple. Here they become victims not only of nefarious arms trading, but also of their own death wish. A final point of contact between the films lies in the respective endings. Marie's painted dancer's face is a mask of grief, a mark of permanent mourning. After killing Marianne, Ferdinand paints himself a blue face, like an early Picasso clown – Pierrot le fou. For Marie the mask conceals permanent mourning, for Pierrot it signifies tragedy as farce, the desperation of the dynamite clown who blows himself up in a gesture of despair.

In the revolution of film form itself, Godard goes further. In her 1966 review of *Pierrot le fou*, Ropars-Wuilleumier pointed out the deep fissure that had appeared between image and narration and which becomes embodied in the figures of the two lovers, the contradiction between a filmic language of poetry and the narrative demand for temporal flow. 'Marianne lives in time', she claimed, 'while Ferdinand contemplates space'. But by adopting only Ferdinand's point of view, that of poetry, Godard is condemned to being led by a narration he cannot control' (Ropars-Wuilleumier 2000:181). Here, by mixing Bergman with film noir, he cannot fully reproduce what he revered in Bergman: a filmmaking of the instant, where by seizing the present at its most fugitive (which the archipelago passion does), Bergman delivers 'the quality of eternity' (Milne 1986:85). Genre intervenes and pulls back from the eternity of the instant that poetry seeks, and substitutes the zigzag flow of a pastiche plot in which Marianne has involved her lover. Godard's cinema of poetry, filtered through the voice and figure of Ferdinand, is bookended by the dictates of noir, the breathless getaway reversed by the fatal double-cross. Eternity on this view is a brief interlude in the incessant flow of movement, the hyper-modernity of time.

The last key link lies in repetition, and pays explicit homage to *Summer with Monika*. Over halfway through *Pierrot le fou* Karina repeats the look to camera that famously defined Andersson's Monika (over halfway through Bergman's film). For Godard the critic, the Monika stare was more than just a smart reflexive gimmick, it was an existential homage to the presence of the camera and the origin of a trope now wrongly taken as postmodern pastiche. Yet he also saw it as more than just a knowing sign of the coming treachery, where Monika is set to return to the foul older lover she knew before Harry. 'Her laughing eyes clouded with confusion', Godard wrote, '[she] calls on us to witness her disgust at involuntarily choosing hell instead of heaven'. It was a bold committed statement from a young critic (ibid.). In *Pierrot* Marianne's double stare to camera was a bold committed shot, a succinct variation on Monika, forcing the viewer to query the delicate balance in his femme fatale between loyalty and duplicity. Outside the island cottage where they prepare to eat, Pierrot seeks reassurance that she will never leave him. Godard cuts from his preferred medium-long shots to a rare close-up. Marianne glances at Pierrot and replies 'of course not', then turns and looks straight to camera. She then repeats the words and the gesture a second time to signify duplicity – the 'of course not' addressed to him, then the swivel of the head and second look straight to camera. Marianne thus 'doubles' the Monika look in Bergman as if her betrayal was doubly intense, her repetition proof of the lover's lie delivered with a sudden glow of self-abasement. And like Bergman, there is no escape from the face whose look to camera lingers in defiance…

Bergman in Paris: 'Marta's Tale' in *Waiting Women*

If *Cahiers* was lured by the Stockholm archipelago, then Bergman, briefly at the start of the 1950s, had been lured by Paris – and it was very much the next stage on his road to autonomy and vitality. So let us go back to the film right after *Summer Interlude* that reunited Maj-Britt Nilsson and Birger Malmsten: *Waiting Women*. In a story of three flashbacks about the love lives of three women – sisters-in-law – linked by a framing device and by marriage to three Lobelius brothers, the Paris in question is in the second story flashback, related by Marta (Nilsson) about her first meeting with unpredictable husband Martin (Malmsten). Bergman's reuse of the Maj/Birger combo is a great success. While the tale starts at the Lobelius summer house in the archipelago, it involved a triple location shoot: the island, Stockholm and then Paris. Bergman's city locations around the Seine, Montmartre and the Bois de Boulogne were focused and precise, and more effervescent than anything he had previously filmed in Stockholm or Malmö. The episode was also testament to the elusive powers of memory. His images were striving to code memories as cinematic signs – the second time since *Summer Interlude* that his flashback technique had produced something extraordinary and deeply mysterious. In *Summer Interlude* the memory image had been simple and streamlined. Here it is ambitious, complex and transforming.

It is also unexpected, for the film does not start well. Another early Bergman-stasis, this time with the Lobelius wives whiling away the time waiting for the return of their husbands from Copenhagen, and a first flashback tale that collects all the Bergman clichés to date (and some to come): first wife's soporific affair with young handsome guy, much older husband's suicidal horror on being told, melodrama drowning the dialogue, fake emotional climax and unconvincing reconciliation at the end. Thus far, your heart is in your mouth. But Marta's tale brought to life by Nilsson is something else. While the film's format and flashbacks seem to be taken hastily from Mankiewicz's *A Letter to Three Wives* (1949), the mellifluous flashback-within-flashback form of Marta's tale is more akin to David Lean's *The Passionate Friends* (1948), a sensuous melodrama of the same year set in London and Switzerland with Ann Todd in the starring role. Through Todd's memory of a past affair that returns to haunt her, Lean's film folds back fluently into the past with its own poetic rhythms and fascination. Bergman does likewise, using his own version of the double flashback. Marta first recalls her difficult pregnancy, then recalls her mind flashing further back under anaesthetic to her fateful meeting in Paris with the father of her future (and then unwanted) child. Here it is not so much in the substance, but in the ambitious telling of the tale that Bergman finally hits the mark. The Paris of his imagination confirms him as a truly original filmmaker.

Let us look more closely. Heavily pregnant and feeling her first contractions, the father-to-be nowhere in sight, Marta packs her suitcase for the hospital. Unable to contact a taxi from her apartment, she prepares for a long walk. In her apartment hallway on the other side of the frosted door-pane is a smudged male figure she – and we – can briefly identify as Death, an apparition which echoes the appearance of the old woman Marie had seen on her return to the island in *Summer Interlude*. There could be a simple explanation – a passing neighbour or a salesman who decides at the last moment not to call. But the outline without a face is ominous, a portent, a sign of something else – the fear of death in childbirth that marks the difficult passage of a new life. As she walks alone through deserted city streets to the hospital, the setting is surreal in its look. Bergman uses intense midsummer light to create high contrast between vivid whiteness and dark tree shadow. Long black shadows striate the bright white streets on the diagonal as Marta strides through them in a quick montage of overhead shots, which nonetheless makes her journey seem endless. The sequence prefigures Isak Borg's opening dream in *Wild Strawberries* with its midsummer light, its bright coffin and its eyeless Figure of Death. Marta's flashback turns six years later into Isak's nightmare. And her memory is of life on a knife edge: birth, renewal, the future all depend on the throw of a dice. As the delivery gets more difficult in the hospital, Bergman intercuts the primary flashbacks – reminiscences of painful labour with gas mask and then full anaesthetic – with further fevered flashbacks from the hospital bed that spiral backwards as if searching for the moment of conception, its primal scene in Paris and the romantic lover who has fathered the (unwanted) child about to emerge from her womb. It is exquisite lyrical composition and Bergman's most powerful summoning of time past before *Wild Strawberries*.

Bergman's vision of Paris is ambivalent. It is a lover's city with its own magnetic aura, but it has that archetypal decadence in its cabaret sequence with its bare-breasted dancers and sexual flaunting that is a postwar provocation. Paris is not Stockholm, but neither is it Hollywood. Bergman knew full well his cabaret sequence would have been too risqué for Hollywood, but he also codes his difference with things American through the figure of the naïve, arrogant USAF officer; a silent figure glibly drawing up house plans for his future life with Marta at the nightclub, while she to his horror, takes up an onstage offer for a contest in which she must grip a coin between her thighs. The parody is obvious: Paris may be a touch too decadent, but the new conquerors of Europe are too puritan. Bergman's sly dig at uniformed Americana also makes a virtue of necessity. This is part of a long wordless sequence using the découpage of silent film, where Bergman does not need English dialogue or American accents. Yet the taxi sequence outside the club, where Marta finally escapes the American's clutches, is like a running gag from a 1920s Hollywood comedy. Bergman thus pays homage and undermines it at the same time.

We might want to contrast Bergman's silent American male with Godard's loquacious American female, Jean Seberg's Patricia – very different versions of an American in Paris, yet both versions of 'the wrong lover'. Marta escapes by abandoning her brash American and falling for a Swedish romantic. Godard's Michel remains fixated on his American lover: his failure to abandon her leads to his downfall. Bergman's GI is an arrogant fool: Godard's Patricia an apparent naïf and yet very much a variation on the femme fatale of Preminger's *Bonjour Tristesse* (1958), from which Godard had plucked Seberg for his debut feature. 'Marta's Tale' is about a transfer of allegiance that ends in marriage; Michel's tale is about a continuing obsession that ends in death. Yet there is a key feature in Marta we later find in Godard's women – the female transfer of affection. That same motif later shows in *Summer with Monika* and the Bibi Andersson of past and present in *Wild Strawberries*, the sweetheart stolen from him in Isak Borg's memory-world by his brother and her update, her contemporary double: the flirting hitchhiker in the backseat of his daughter's car playing off two male buddies against each other. No wonder then that the theme of the woman with two lovers found fertile ground in Godard's Paris. In his short film 'Montparnasse and Levaillois' for the New Wave *Paris vu par* collection of 1965, the Canadian actress Joanna Shimkus played Monika, the girl with two boyfriends, in clear homage to Bergman's film. Godard, typically, replaces the idyllic archipelago with a noisy Parisian workshop. Nothing could be further from Bergman – and yet so near at the same time.

In Marta's tale her new love, the awkward Swedish 'artist' in Paris, is coded as a double of Bergman himself. In the nightclub sequence the flirtatious Martin, who is sending Marta messages via the waiter, is first seen full face in the reflection of her makeup mirror as she freshens up her face, heard later but not seen outside the door of her apartment, then barely seen at all until seduction takes place inside. Later in a hotel lobby, Bergman makes a signature appearance – in a wall mirror in long shot behind Marta as she tidies herself before leaving to see her new lover. Again like Malmsten, reflection before image. Bergman's trademark beret and loose bohemian jacket are there for all to see before he vanishes. Two fleeting mirror images: Bergman and his screen alter ego, both elusive, the romantic 'artist' who may or may not adapt to fatherhood, the exile who may or may not come home (Martin eventually does because he is broke). Here the film is better when Malmsten is silent and when he is seen in fragments. Thus Bergman builds up the suspense to the flirtation by creating partial images of Marta's future lover, his thin, reedy voice first heard in the song by which he serenades her through the apartment door. Yes, it is corny but still a worthwhile suspense of withholding, for thereafter the best sequences of the infatuated lovers are wordless, a montage of locations in which the warm Parisian sun dazzles the waters of the Seine and the lake in the Bois de Boulogne. The moulding of Malmsten as a silent figure here works intermittently through romantic idiom. When Bergman returns to the device in *The Silence*, the mood is grimly post-romantic: the wannabe artist is replaced by the hedonistic waiter, love replaced by lust and enchantment by darkness. Nothing could be more different from the way Malmsten playfully picks up Nilsson in the Parisian club and the way ten years later he ruthlessly picks up Gunnel Lindblom in the Timoka city café where he serves her.

In Marta's tale the lure of Paris is clear, the springboard that inspired Bergman to experiment anew with images, flashback, montage and wordless sound sequence. He himself notes the movie origin of the experiment lay elsewhere, in the wordless narrative sequences of Czech director Gustave Machatý's *Extase* (1933), remembered for its nude bathing scene with Hedy Lamarr and its stunning pastoral sequences (Bergman 1995:291). Yet here Bergman is also inspired by Paris to explore the landscape within the cityscape as a prelude to that masterly fusion in *Wild Strawberries* where he blends country and city as dreamscapes in the journey of Isak Borg. Before that he persisted with the 'silence' experiment in his bittersweet 1955 feature *Dreams* and its inspired opening. We can note the length of the wordless fashion photo shoot at the start, which he then extends indirectly to the next major sequence, the wordless montage of the train journey to Gothenberg where Susanne, the fashion editor (Eva Dahlbeck), contemplates suicide by jumping out of the carriage door. Yet while lacking the magic of Marta's flashback, with its layers of the past unfolding as images of desire, the train journey south is brilliantly atmospheric and establishes something that *Waiting Women* lacked – the spatial continuum of movement towards that echoes the earlier train journey back to Sweden from Switzerland in *Three Strange Loves*. Soon *Wild Strawberries* would combine the best of both of these things, the movement forward in space (*Three Strange Loves, Dreams*) with the oneiric movement backward in time (*Summer Interlude, Waiting Women*); the car journey south (to Lund) with the delirium of Borg's memory that takes us back to the start of the century. Yet, as we shall see, it was *Dreams* that fascinated Eric Rohmer and fed into his conceiving of the *conte moral*, the moral tale.

Godard in Sweden: ·*The Silence, A Married Woman, Masculine-Feminine*

Just as Bergman made one film partly in Paris, Godard made *Masculine-Feminine* partly in Sweden, a condition of that film's co-production finance. Bergman, you feel, made his episode to salute the romance of Paris: making a virtue of financial necessity. Godard, you feel, made a perverse salute to the impact of Bergman. Bergman's Paris shoot had been a lengthy shoot of a long episode, one of three. Godard's brevity is a single episode, one of fifteen, credited in the intertitles as episode 11 and featuring the Swedish shoot as a film within a film, a 'foreign' movie that Paul (Jean-Pierre Léaud) and his girl friends watch intermittently in a Paris cinema. Godard's cinema-film is nothing like Bergman's Paris excursion, except for one small thing. Both portray a passionate encounter in a foreign country by using Birger Malmsten. In Godard of course the romance has gone, for *The Silence* had intervened. This is his variation on a lustful, wordless encounter in a foreign city, openly satirical. Whereas the silence of *The Silence* is gripping and oppressive, Godard's spoof on wordless desire (and on Malmsten) features grunts, groans and anxious lust. But we should remember how talky Godard's films are by contrast and this one in particular. Hence the attraction of opposites: silent Malmsten set against loquacious Léaud, unlikely doubles in film history.

Episode 11 remains ambivalent, for it is filtered through a film Godard truly admired (number two on his top ten list for 1962) and which he had also used as a template for *A Married Woman*. This reflexive filter of difference – difference in vision, difference in modernisms, in effect difference in cinema – contains opposing variations on Bergman, stylistic imitation in *A Married Woman*, and mischievous satire in *Masculine-Feminine*, where he is satirizing not only Bergman but also himself for copying his Nordic predecessor in the earlier film. It is as if Bergman already had shown Godard, through his transformation of Malmsten (from naïve lover in *Summer Interlude* to ruthless seducer of *The Silence*), the way in which his films could be copied and parodied. The parody itself, seen in bits onscreen, is largely juvenile and, taken as a sum of the segments of the film within the film, inconsequential. But here Godard is not interested in the 'Swedish' film per se. He is interested in the way he discontinuously cuts it into his own film. The sequence is a key instance of his modernist aesthetic, his montage of distractions, a film form constantly distracting the spectator from its core narrative by action forever moving sideways and only incidentally forward. Moreover Léaud's hyperactive 'acting', in effect the acting out of his own persona, instantly fits the bill. As the screening takes place he twice leaves the auditorium, first to go to the men's room where he sees a gay couple kissing in a cubicle, the second time to charge round to the projection room where he accuses the projectionist of showing the film in the wrong screen ratio. As well as reverse angles to Léaud's watching the crowd murmuring about the film, what we can call swift interruptions, there are the slow interruptions of Léaud's two mini-adventures. Godard thus establishes a fast–slow ratio of interrupting the flow of the film within the film. But of course we don't know if there is any flow in what he shot in Sweden. A thirty-something couple go back to what appears to be a hotel room and enact a seduction rite where grunts and groans replace words, a silent sequence shown in snatches with occasional sound effects. The Parisian audience is blank and so are we, watching them watching as Godard's self-conscious modernism finds its degree zero in the antics of his freak onscreen couple.

And yet there is a link to an earlier scene in *Pierrot le fou*, where Belmondo dozes off in a cinema while watching Jean Seberg in Godard's unreleased Moroccan short *Le Grand escroc* (1963). Léaud without knowing it is watching his screen double, once the young bohemian of a previous generation, just as Belmondo 'without knowing it' is failing to watch his leading, treacherous lady from *Breathless*, in a movie where he is again soon betrayed. Both are tongue-in-cheek instances of non-recognition. And just as Malmsten plays second fiddle to Nilsson and to Bergman in both their Bergman films together, so Léaud as Paul plays second fiddle to his director, not as a Bergman 'coat-hanger' but by acting out 'himself': a hyperactive manchild as the figure-filter through whom Godard orchestrates his quasi-film. Student Malmsten had been lamely romantic: student Léaud is a cipher of the post-romantic. Godard perversely undermines the residues of his troubled romanticism through this figure of hyperactive enchantment. Here Léaud's vitality comes from two things – constant distraction from purpose and constant evasion of feeling, mainly through pontificating about political attitudes and fashioning absurd notions of sexual difference. It is a Godardian ploy to create pathos through evasion. In Bergman there is no pontificating and no evasion. The camera on the face is unflinching, the naked exposure of distressed feeling relentless, even when the meaning of feeling is enigmatic or ambiguous. Even when elusive, Bergman's pathos is somehow organic. Godard in *Masculine-Feminine* is trying to put the genie back in the bottle: it is in its own way, a very Calvinist film. If Bergman's *Winter Light,* which Godard had so admired, was the extreme end of Lutheranism – suppression of shame and guilt through suffocation of words and feelings – then the anxieties of Léaud that register through evasion and distraction seem to be those in a secular world of not knowing whether or not one is damned. The ostensible Marxist angst flagged up in the hero's scattergun discourse – am I on the right side of the class struggle? – seems to work as a complex variation on the Calvinist dilemma of damnation. Hyperactive movement, incessant talk, exhortation to revolution – are they the provisional signs of salvation where none are given?

The prehistory of Godard's Swedish film within the film lies not only in *The Silence* but also in *A Married Woman,* which had been shot and edited with breathtaking speed in the summer of 1964, as Godard later acknowledged in his Montreal lecture series of 1977. But let's reprise the Stockholm fragment of *Masculine-Feminine.* Godard films the first part in lengthy takes using medium-long shots, very Godardian, very New Wave, and the second part – of the couple's embrace – in satirical close shots reminiscent of the close-ups in both *The Silence* and *A Married Woman.* In *A Married Woman* the lovers' kiss and the close shot are both frequent. In *Masculine-Feminine,* Godard the Calvinist is happy to show Léaud in bed with three women, but is loathe to film close embrace. Malmsten is another matter. The sudden cut to his contorted kiss in extreme close-up in the Stockholm fragment is the one amusing shot in the whole sequence, parodically anti-romantic. The actor's face in the act of kissing is grotesquely distorted in a convex mirror giving him a magnified eye, so that the contact of lovers' lips is made to look wonderfully ridiculous. The image would not have been lost on his watching Parisian double, Léaud, if indeed Léaud had bothered to look, which he does not. His Swedish double from a previous generation appears distinctly uncool: no wonder then that Léaud doesn't recognize him.

A Married Woman we could say is halfway between *To Live My Life* (1962) and *Masculine-Feminine.* It sustained what Godard inherits from Bergman but what also defines Truffaut's intriguing *Soft Skin* (1964) from the previous year, the existential uncertainties of infidelity. But it also crosses that theme with the concern marking Godard's next series of films, the mythologies of mass consumer discourse. Its hotel passion echoes the betrayal of Ester by Anna in *The Silence*, but Godard opts for abstraction, consumerism and city life as opposed to the virtual world of Bergman's film – a world it seems, on the verge of war. Godard's locations are diverse and recognisably Parisian: Bergman's foreign city, Timoka, was a studio build at Råsunda (Koskinen 2010:28). In the context of the New Wave, Brody suggests Godard's facility in matching contradictory philosophies, the structuralist themes of mass consumerism (courtesy of Barthes and Levi-Strauss) with the existentialism of Sartre, is one of the Parisian film's main achievements (Brody 2008:190). The love triangle also had autobiographical overtones. Charlotte (Macha Méril) married with a young child, is having a secret affair with an actor (Bernard Noël) at a time in Godard's personal life when his wife Anna Karina, also with a young child, was having an affair with actor Maurice Ronet (ibid.:196). Just as we could say that in *The Silence* the adventures and lust of Anna are seen through the jealous eyes of her sister Ester, so here the camera distances itself from the affair through the nervous, backward glances of Charlotte, who is convinced that private investigators are tracking her treachery on behalf of her husband. In Bergman however the approach is very different. With the sisters stranded in a foreign city and Anna's young son Johan as bemused intermediary, the use of the close shot on the passionate body demonstrates the unbearable closeness of being. Ester and Anna, even while hating each other, cannot escape each other. In Godard's examination of the cheating couple, the close shot used against the blank canvas of white sheets or white walls, seems at first the very opposite, emotionless, a mere tool for deconstructing body parts. Godard's self-proclaimed 'fragments of a film' that mark the opening credits are turned in the film itself into fragments of the cheating body – legs, arms, head, torso, belly. And yet there is an abstract beauty to this segmental filming, so that dissection inadvertently becomes instant recomposition. Instead of dissolving faithlessness through knowing style, Godard affirms it inadvertently through aesthetic beauty. He moves the 'independent girl' of Bergman's early cinema into the autonomous woman of the New Wave. While Truffaut's vision of faithlessness was quasi-tragic – in *Jules and Jim* (1962), *Soft Skin* (to which Godard is responding here), *Mississippi Mermaid* (1969) and *The Woman next Door* (1981) – in Godard's film life goes on and Macha Méril commands the screen not as a tragic, transgressive figure but as a woman and mother genuinely torn between husband and lover.

Nose to Nose or Eye to Lip: Variations on the Tandem Shot

We have already looked at Godard's reframing in *Pierrot le fou* of Harriet Andersson's prolonged look to camera in *Monika*. We can now turn to another – a first for Bergman – the tandem close-up, nose to nose, of the sisters in Ester's hotel room in *The Silence*. Godard's reprise of this innovative shot comes in the scene between the two lovers at the end of *A Married Woman*, also staged in a hotel room, this time at Orly airport. As noted, *Masculine-Feminine*'s spoof on the Bergman close-up had also been a send-up of Godard's use of the close shot in *A Married Woman*. Satire is a hair's breadth from homage, which in turn merges with autocritique. But do the almost identical tandem close-ups in Bergman and in *A Married Woman*, where no satire is intended, share the same emotional meaning?

In her close study of the continuity script for *The Silence*, Koskinen has discovered that corrections and drawings were made for the key hotel room sequence, which revealed a sudden move away from conventional over-the-shoulder close shots to a landmark tandem two shot with an added instruction, not previously featured in Bergman's filming, a 'nose-to-nose' staging. She suggests that its sudden placement could signify a wholeness, a unity between the two sisters that is, 'only momentary and provisional, and a moment of grace' (Koskinen 2010:134). It seems to me that it can be seen as a moment of grace precisely because it portends subsequent separation; the very closeness at that point of Ester (Ingrid Thulin) and Anna (Gunnel Lindblom) suggests the final ending of their incestuous affair. Bergman partly naturalizes the staging. The tandem close-up is also a window shot, with Anna looking out at the street in profile and Ester in full face behind, watching her looking out. Ester, in other words, is watching her sister intently while Anna is refusing to look back, even if the camera placement suggests their faces are nearly touching. The ninety-degree angle on facial placement, nose to nose, gives us the focused gaze of the lover at close quarters, on the vacant look of the beloved, who is about to confess betrayal. The jealous Ester has already spotted Anna's stained summer dress and smelt the semen on it after it has been discarded. Anna then confesses her witnessing of the lovemaking couple at the cabaret and her consequent seduction by the waiter, though deviously, since she gives two conflicting accounts of the seduction – one of which she then disowns as a 'lie'. The confession is not a prelude to forgiveness or reconciliation. Anna is about to rejoin the waiter for an extended bout of lovemaking in a room they have booked on the other side of the hotel corridor.

Later that night in the rented room of the two lovers, Bergman repeats the tandem shot through the visual symmetry of reversing the placement. Having been told by Johan, Anna's son, of the couple in the room, Ester surprises them after their lovemaking seems exhausted. Ester moves to the foot of the bed, Anna heaves herself forward to confront her sister – cue the second tandem shot. This time the profile is to the left of the screen, not the right; and it is Ester's profile, not Anna's. Standing by the window nothing had separated them: now they are brutally bisected by the huge rails at the end of the bedstead, which Anna grasps with aggressive hands, staring at her sister, so near and yet so far. As Anna stares, Ester looks away. The look of love (Ester on Anna) is replaced by the look of hate (Anna on Ester), but hatred at a price. Anna's look and words of hate are undercut by her recognition of the final loss of love, the mutual abjection into which her desire has plunged both sisters. The waiter watches, biding his time, not understanding their verbal language but recognizing body language all too well. As Ester leaves, he drags his prey back down into bed with him. In placing these two tandem shots in sequences just before and just after the furtive lovemaking, Bergman's aesthetic blends the symmetries of inversion – visual and emotional. Image and feeling merge. They become identical.

If Bergman's tandem shots are before-and-after staging, extended in their duration, Godard's tandems in the penultimate sequence of *A Married Woman* are swift and consecutive. Visual reversal follows immediately. It is the instance of the lover's first separation from Charlotte as he leaves for a performance of Racine's *Bérénice* in Marseilles, part of a rather different hotel room staging, which Godard places at Orly airport: love in the afternoon for an hour before departure, and brightly lit where Bergman's hotel rooms had been dark and brooding. The tandem shots form part of a mosaic of body fragments – lovers' hands washing in the same bowl, legs caressing, lips on flesh, a montage of poetic fragments that earlier Godard had matched to fragments of Charlotte's voiceover. Here he inserts the tandems in extreme close-up, moving from Bergman's measured nose-to-nose composition in full face, to right-angle fragments of the magnified face – from lip to eye and eye to lip. He does not alter the lovers' positions in the symmetry of reversal, but merely speaker and listener and the angle of the shot. In the first shot the lover frontally looks to camera with his left eye alone in frame, while Charlotte in profile above looks to the lover, whispering 'I love you'. As she does so, she pulls down the lower lid of his staring eye, creating comic distortion in his one-eyed look to camera. In the second shot, the lover still faces the camera with Charlotte in profile but this time we see his lips, not his eyes, framed between his nose above and Charlotte's nose below and it is his turn to say 'I love you'. The double decentring of composition, where each character in turn has lips but no eyes, is Godard's effacement of the entire face (Koskinen 2010:135–56), where the detached focus on facial fragments undermines the double declaration of love and severs the connections of words and images. It is a study in the art of misalignment, a near Cubist image, denying Bergman's 'moment of grace'. Again it is a portent of things to come. Closeness signifies separation. The relationship in both cases will soon be over, but in Bergman and not in Godard, you sense it has been a liaison of explosive passion. While Bergman focuses on the feeling contained in the look – the feeling that practically shatters the look – Godard focuses self-consciously, almost quizzically on the look itself, magnified to the very edge of clear sight, an inch from dissolving into nothingness.

In the prelude to his tandem shots, Godard differs from Bergman in two vital respects. He naturalizes his exterior setting with Coutard using a long wheelchair dolly as the couple leave the Orly cinema (where, incredibly, they have watched Resnais' *Night and Fog*) and walk their discreet and separate ways towards the nearby hotel. The staging is fluid, matter-of-fact and softly comic. Bergman's lovers, by contrast, edge along a dimly lit corridor in a Råsunda film studio interior: they are spotted by Johan who is lurking in the shadows. The waiter rattles the key desperately in the lock, trying to turn it. The staging is dramatic, expressive, uncanny. Godard shoots on location to create the illusion of transparency; Bergman in the studio to create the illusion of opacity. At the same time the opposite occurs. Bergman lures us in compellingly with the close shot to create suspension of disbelief, and in the two tandem shots his actors are at their best, his staging is at its boldest and strongest. Illusion and emotion merge. In the hotel room Godard, however, dispenses with Bergman's medium close-up and long interior takes to create swift body montage in which two tandem shots are inserted in extreme close-up, shattering the suspension of disbelief. Both are triumphant risk-taking strategies. In his shooting of body fragments on white surfaces, bed sheets, pillows and white walls, Godard also anticipates the abstractions of *Persona*. To be glacial is to be beautiful. Meanwhile *The Silence*'s hotel rooms and corridors are shadowy and labyrinthine. We are in a strange world, but so close in, so involved, the desire to exit is replaced by the desire to linger. For us to chose Bergman over Godard or Godard over Bergman is a perilous act indeed because at the end of the day, or more precisely by the end of the century, we are truly spoilt for choice. And yet there is an implacable sense that Godard completely escaped Bergman's influence and became a director the Swede would not recognize. Bergman's verdict on the Swiss cineaste in 2002: 'Endless, dull, Godard is desperately boring. I've always thought he made films for the critics. He made a movie here in Sweden, *Masculin-Féminin*, that was so boring it made my hair stand on end' (Aghed 2007:197). A case, perhaps, of the sorcerer's apprentice?

Truffaut and the Woman-in-Trouble: *Through a Glass Darkly* and *The Story of Adèle H.*

Like the rest of the New Wave, Truffaut had no special attachment to Bergman's costume dramas or his metaphysics. His interest was contemporary. Yet he shared with Godard a fascination with the way in which a male director like Bergman created such dominating female roles. 'His female characters', Truffaut observed, 'are infinitely subtle while his male characters are conventions' (Truffaut 1980:258). In the 1960s films another tendency had come to the fore: the absolute priority of the face (ibid.:259), which in effect is the female face. Before he made *The Story of Adèle H.* (1975), his loose biography of Victor Hugo's little-known daughter starring Isabelle Adjani, Truffaut had time to absorb the use of the face and the use of colour in *Cries and Whispers*, which he rightly predicted would be Bergman's biggest box-office hit since *The Silence*; (shrewdly, Truffaut realized both films lured audiences into their emotional drama without the puzzling abstractions of *Persona*). Stylistically *Adèle H.* is close to the *Kammerspiel* intimacy of both, but if anything a near immediate response to *Cries and Whispers*: one history film to another – Bergman's turn of century, Truffaut's nearer mid nineteenth century, and one colour film to another, both with clear restriction of the colour spectrum – Bergman with saturated whites, reds and blacks, Truffaut with faded autumnal colours.

Thematically and emotionally, however, it is closer to Bergman's first *Kammerspiel* film *Through a Glass Darkly*, in its focus on a vulnerable woman whose life borders on madness, inseparable from an enclosed family life. This is the single film of both directors about a woman spiritually alone that ends in the onset of insanity. In Bergman's contemporary film with Harriet Andersson as Karin, the madness erupts in and through the presence of the family. But in Truffaut's loose biopic, the madness erupts in and through the absent presence of the family. The difference is crucial, but one film flows from the other. In

Bergman's film there is a literal cast of four – all come together on holiday at their island summerhouse: father, son, daughter, daughter's husband; while *Adèle H.* has a core virtual quartet – lonely daughter in the New World, absent father in the Old World, sister Léopoldine dead by drowning, and a desired 'husband', Lieutenant Pinson, present and incorrect, who refuses to marry her. Both fathers are celebrity novelists (one invented, one real), and both siblings too close for comfort: Karin's teenage brother in close sensual proximity, Adèle's dead sister lingering on in dreams and nightmares. Both films are austerely Nordic. Bergman's was the real thing, shot for the first time on the island of Fårö with natural summer light, usually at dawn or dusk. Truffaut's staging was virtual 'Nordic', using Guernsey as a stand-in for Halifax, Nova Scotia and usually shooting in darkness to fabricate a claustrophobic look that is often deemed 'Nordic' in appearance. Bergman's film was the second feature, after *The Virgin Spring*, of cinematographer Sven Nykvist, whose visual eye was indispensable for the director's new *Kammerspiel* aesthetic in the years to come.

An inversion in the look of the heroine and the contrast it generates should also be noted. In Bergman's monochrome picture, Karin's dresses are summery, pale or white; the clothes of her male family dark or black. In Halifax, Adèle wears a drab brown bonnet and shawl in keeping with her incognito status, while Pinson (Bruce Robinson) sports a military uniform with gold braid and dashing red stripes. In both films, we feel the intimacy with the 'husband'– real or virtual – is overshadowed by the liaison with the father, and the father is the prime source of feelings of rejection. Karin discovers her father's notebooks, which reveal him cynically using her as a case history for his latest piece of fiction. Adèle feels passed over in favour of her older sister Léopoldine, whose tragic death by drowning had produced a public cult of mourning in France. The memory of the dead daughter seems, to her eyes, more potent for the great author than the absence of the living one on the other side of the Atlantic. If Bergman's 1960 film is a defining moment for a new form of *Kammerspiel* modernism, then Truffaut's 1975 film seems to signify its dispersal, two years after *Cries and Whispers*. Two of the family quartet are simply not there in the flesh; the third – indifferent ex-lover and virtual husband – is not there in spirit. Adèle is thus a woman alone, endowed with the materiality of lone presence, but simultaneously robbed of any sense of presence through non-identity: a woman whose identity can only be sealed, if at all, by others who will not or cannot do it; a woman who does not know who she is, and wants to escape the tyranny of her own name 'Hugo', with the titular name of her preferred husband 'Pinson' or 'Penson' as she calls him (Gillain 1991). The film thus traces the self-delusionary journey from being 'Adèle H.' to being 'Mrs Penson'.

With Truffaut, you sense an openness in Adèle's fate that had not been present in Bergman's rendering of Karin's schizophrenia. For with Karin the illness is sealed in, doomed to repeat itself, and yet the film around it is not strong enough in its tight bourgeois setting to suggest classical tragedy. Instead there percolates throughout a Langian sense of fatality, and Bergman gives us the intimate chronicle of a doom foretold. The fiction had a historical precedent in another famous novelist with a troubled daughter: the sad story of James and Claudia Joyce – the eminent father's talented offspring, who could read *Finnegan's Wake* but not live in the real world of Joyce's exile. She was confined to an asylum for most of her adult life, a fate that appears to await Karin at the end of Bergman's film. Hugo–Joyce–Bergman: a fascinating triple. Yet while the Joyce world was embroiled in the vexed relationship between language and life, the vexed Bergman relationship here is between the world of the human and the world of the divine. Moreover, there is no final miracle as there was in Dreyer's *Ordet*. For Karin, divine visitation is inseparable from schizophrenic voices that command her actions. Her God is finally a malevolent God who comes to her in the form of a black spider, violating her in her physical and spiritual nakedness. Adèle's final illness is very different: it reveals itself in the dusty streets of Barbados, not as a monstrous recognition of the divine, but as delirious non-recognition of the English lieutenant. After she has tailed Pinson to Barbados and the blinding white heat of the Caribbean, she fails to recognize him in the street and walks on by. While Karin's is an act of false recognition of the 'beloved', Adèle's is non-recognition of the ex-lover. Both fixations explode by contrary means and in their wake bring the void of madness.

Bergman and Rohmer: The Mirage and the Moral Tale

We could say that Bergman's archipelago movies, stories of a summer island break, are echoed throughout Rohmer's long career in his various vacation movies: *The Collector* (1967), *Claire's Knee* (1970), *Pauline at the Beach* (1983), *The Green Ray* (1986), *A Summer Tale* (1996) and more. Yet in 'Bergmanorama', Rohmer had focused on one specific picture that was not an archipelago film but still proved to be a significant influence on his own cinema. This was Bergman's contemporary

1955 fable *Dreams*, of a train journey by two women in the fashion industry from Stockholm to Gothenburg for a photo shoot (experienced photographer Susanne played by Eva Dahlbeck and young model Doris by Harriet Andersson). Here they have contrasting encounters that are quasi-romantic, but they end up back in Stockholm in very much the same position they started out. Doris, the ditzy young model, is reconciled with her student boyfriend after a surreal encounter with a wealthy older diplomat. Susanne tries in vain to restart her affair with a married businessman and ends up single and alone again. The motif of this film echoes throughout Rohmer's second series of the 1980s, *Comedies and Proverbs*. The parallel lives of the younger and the older woman, romantically speaking, are reprised by Rohmer in, for example, *Pauline at the Beach*. The abrupt curtailment of the brief encounter, seen from the female point of view, is reprised in *A Good Marriage* (1982) with the young Béatrice Romand. What Rohmer takes up at a deeper level, however, are the vital textures of Bergman's film – the incongruence of romantic mismatch, the abrupt curtailment of the faltering liaison, along with the ridicule and humiliation that surrounds it: all elements, in effect, of a thin dividing line from the spectator's point of view, between comic irony and moral judgment. Should we chuckle at vaguely amusing disappointments of the heart, or should we, through them, make wider judgments about the human condition?

Often referred to by its alternate title, *Journey into Autumn*, the Swedish original of *Dreams* is *Kvinnodröm* or literally 'women's dreams'. Here is the origin for Bergman, who liked making train movies, of the filmic dream journey that marks out *Wild Strawberries* and *The Silence*. To view the film naturalistically works on a single plane, for sure, but excludes the oneiric elements that make the narrative more enticing, the ghostliness of the women's parallel encounters. These are simultaneously staged as real and dreamlike events, all the more so for their use of locations and naturalistic framing. At the film's very start Bergman breaks with sound naturalism by abolishing dialogue in two near wordless sequences – the fashion shoot, followed by the night train journey to Gothenburg. In the first sequence, fat journal editor Magnus, stuck in his canvas chair, tapping his chubby, ringed finger as the shoot with Doris progresses, may well be an effigy of Hitchcock, whom Bergman, though an admirer, thought too sedentary for his own good. With its swift parallel editing of misted windows, speeding rails, distraught close-ups and warning signs, the train montage, where Susanne ponders jumping from the speeding express, is a brilliant imitation of Hitchcock's use of montage for dramatic suspense. Bergman is thus wrong-footing his audience; what starts out as a

Hitchcock movie soon becomes a Bergman film. Thereafter, as Rohmer points out: 'These two women's dreams are shown each time in the form of an *intoxication*, in which, through the exaltation of sounds and images, the director wants us to participate' (Rohmer 1989:164–65).

The intoxication of the event, the adrenalin rush of the impossible encounter, are what define the day in Gothenburg for both women. What also defines it are the outcomes: the reality check, where the intervention of a triumphant rival deflates their 'dreams'. Susanne's secret hotel room assignation with her bald lover is disrupted by the sudden appearance of his knowing wife; Doris's intoxicated flirtation with a man old enough to be her father is aborted by the sudden appearance of the Consul's adult daughter. Both outsider rivals pour scorn on the mismatched couples: a humiliation where Bergman's dialogue is at its sharply acerbic best, and in which the 'dreams' of both mismatched couples are cruelly exposed. The double intervention is a dramatic device that operates within the frame of classical narration – the moral check on seductive misdemeanour that ends the film and creates not exorcism, but lingering pain. The Consul, who has pursued Doris because she resembles a youthful version of his mad wife, is on the receiving end of a curt reprimand from his vengeful daughter. Susanne and her doleful lover, a businessman now bankrupt, are castigated by none other than Marta Lobelius, the heroine of *Waiting Women*, who is just as smart and resilient here. The bitterness, the desolation and the stoicism that rears up out of comic embarrassment, are something outside the realm of Hollywood. The sensibility is European. Rohmer picks up on it and then transforms it in two specific films, both underrated in the context of his career – *Love in the Afternoon* (1972) from the *Moral Tales* and *A Good Marriage* from *Comedies and Proverbs*.

Let us then pursue this remarkable inversion of Bergman. Though Rohmer, like Bergman, also starts his two films with a train journey, his endings are utterly different. In Rohmer's films there is no moral caution delivered onscreen through dramatic intervention of a third party. His endings are open. Whereas Bergman's closure through dramatic censure follows a classical Hollywood model, Rohmer puts the onus squarely on us to judge without mediation. Yet the Bergmanesque ingredients, the sense of humiliation and embarrassment, the air of desperation and 'intoxicated' pursuit of the singular dream, are all there. In *Love in the Afternoon* Frédéric (Bernard Verley) is a family businessman who pursues Chloé (Zouzou) a feisty, offbeat beauty; while in *A Good Marriage* Béatrice Romand, as art historian Sabine, plays a young woman who vainly pursues an eminent lawyer (André

Dussolier), for purposes of marriage. Both pursuits are glaring social mismatches, just like the Consul's embarrassing pursuit of the feckless Doris, and Susanne's impossible pursuit of the wimpish Lobelius. Both end in failure and Rohmer draws out the fatality of that failure as a long diurnal abjection, which is not secret at all but public and transparent. Everybody knows. The Rohmer strategy is straight out of *Dreams*. In Bergman's film the ageing Consul is 'seen' making a fool of himself: openly buying Doris gifts in expensive shops, flirting with her in a café over cakes and hot chocolate, before taking her to the fairground at her behest, where rough rides on the rollercoaster drive him to collapse in the street afterwards. Conversely, Susanne is also 'seen' making a fool of herself while trying not to. She turns into desperate stalker, spying on the posh Lobelius residence at the edge of town. There she is spotted lurking in nearby woods by Marta Lobelius. Phoning his office later from a genteel teashop in town, where the collective gaze of the female clientele is turned disapprovingly towards her, she loudly begs his secretary in vain for an appointment. And finally 'exposed' when the tough Lobelius spouse bursts into her hotel room to humiliate both her and her bald, melancholy lover. He visibly shrinks into the background trying to stay invisible at the window in a long-take three shot, placed between and behind the two women as they go toe to toe and Susanne loses the argument.

Rohmer uses the desperation of the phone call answered by the obstructive secretary in *A Good Marriage*, where Sabine repeatedly tries to contact the suave, unresponsive Edmond. Rohmer goes further in the party sequence, where Edmond turns up late as reluctant guest to a party for a younger crowd at Sabine's family home, and leaves almost immediately. Humiliation is cumulative, as in Bergman, drawn out and unconditional. We squirm in our seats as sympathy gives way to distance, as we insulate ourselves against the embarrassment of the desperate act, male or female: the deluded Consul balancing the self-deluding Susanne; the uncertain Frédéric in *Love in the Afternoon* balancing the zealous Sabine of *A Good Marriage*. The case of Frédéric, whose office secretaries duly note his compulsive pursuit of Chloé, contains more than meets the eye: the humiliation is less than Sabine's, but the pathology more intense. Like the Consul courting Doris, he pursues Chloé though the labyrinth of the city and like the ghostly Consul, who is first seen as a reflection in a shop window, he comes across as a spectral presence, unlikely and uncanny. Both men pursue younger women with a deathly pallor on their cheeks and by using colour, Rohmer contrasts the paleness of Verley's face with his piercing blue eyes – testament to the compulsiveness of his quest. And that quest, though it appears to be shot naturalistically, has many features of a dream; enough to confound Rohmer's critics when they place him, complacently, as an inspired Bazinian realist.

In *Dreams* and the Rohmer films, failure thus takes place under the gaze of others, sometimes implicit, sometimes explicit and that gaze undoubtedly mediates our own as witnesses to an amusing but sorry fate. The prelude to Frédéric's endless pursuit of Chloé also echoes the almost hallucinatory vision of Paris present in Rohmer's previous Paris feature over ten years earlier: *The Sign of Leo* (1959). Before he meets Chloé, the hero has a dream of mass seduction, in which one by one, the previous heroines of Rohmer's *Moral Tales* – Haydée Politoff, Marie-Christine Barrault, Françoise Fabian, Aurora Cornu, Laurence de Monaghan and Béatrice Romand – all submit to his embrace, hypnotized by his magic amulet. Shot on the street in shallow focus, the dream sequence not only looks different from the normal depth of field in the Rohmer exterior, it also has an unusual reflexive element, in which Frédéric becomes a version of the director himself, exerting his magic influence on all the actresses who have previously worked for him. While Bergman makes his usual cameo appearance in *Dreams* in the lobby of the Gothenburg hotel where Susanne and Doris are staying, the sequence here takes the reflexive into New Wave dimensions, where Rohmer is clearly the contemporary of Godard, Rivette and Truffaut. His modernism becomes subtly apparent in other ways too and here it has to be said, Rohmer departs even further from the classical paradigm bequeathed by Bergman's film. This lies in the aesthetic of the offscreen. Where Bergman had offered us the spectral location, Rohmer adds to it something else – the out-of-field, the elsewhere, in which the transparency of what we see happening is offset by the mystery of what might be happening somewhere else.

The single critic to nail the misconception that Rohmer is a default Bazinian devoted to transparency, a misconception happily fostered by Rohmer himself, is Pascal Bonitzer. As an earlier *Cahiers* critic, he had happily shared in the illusion, as it gave post-1968 *Cahiers* the easy chore of deconstructing Rohmer's alleged naïvety by semiological means (Ballard et al. 2010). But Bonitzer's later monograph on the director changed tack entirely. One of Rohmer's great obsessions, he tells us, is to arrive at delivering mystery by the completely external means that cinema offers (Bonitzer 1999:85). There is something beyond the heard and the seen in the nature of the Rohmerian image: what is offscreen is just as significant as what is viewed. This works itself out primarily in the field of mimetic rivalry, which defines passion. For Bonitzer, Rohmerian protagonists are always betrayed figures, but betrayed above all by themselves. Firstly, because they are mistaken about their own desires and secondly, because they are misled by others, whom they take at their word (ibid.:100). This double deception is usually not fatal, however, because they see the world through a blindfold anyway, which inures them to the worst forms of wounding. The absent rival (Maud's husband), or the absent colleague (Hélène's colleague), is blithely overlooked by the Rohmer protagonist at the very moment when their existence is of vital importance. Ignored, nameless and faceless in the eyes of Rohmer's guillible subject, they may well be the key to the destiny of the film. And when they are seen, they are 'seen' but not looked at, either by the protagonist or the spectator. They are neutral recipients of the non-gaze. In *Full Moon in Paris* (1984), Rohmer supplies us with his cruel exception to the efficacy of the blindfold. Louise overlooks the presence of Marianne with Rémi at a party in Paris full of significant players, just as we do, because her introduction is fleeting and inconspicuous. Yet Marianne will turn out to be Rémi's lover, for whom he abandons her when she least expects it. Louise, deluded by the 'freedom' of her existential double life in Paris and the suburbs, is devastated.

For Frédéric the opposite unfolds. When Chloé tells him she has seen Hélène talking affectionately to one of her colleagues on the street, he blithely ignores the remark. When he finally returns to his suburban home, having failed to seduce the willing Chloé after a long tortuous courtship, no declaration of betrayal awaits him – as it later does Louise in *Full Moon*. Instead, there unfolds one of the most passionate and powerful sequences in all of French cinema. Surprised to see him in the middle of the afternoon, Hélène is then overwhelmed with delight and tears and desire, and her sudden plenitude of emotion is utterly transcendent – a stunning performance from Charlotte Verley: it shatters the screen and finally brings the title of the film to life. This is not because Frédéric has finally rejected Chloé, whose presence he appears to care little about anyway, but because he has no animosity towards her; because he is still doggedly affectionate and dependent. Here Rohmer breaks completely with the naturalism of motive and this directs us to question what we have really seen during the course of his film. Why is Hélène so lacking in suspicion and jealousy, so easy-going about her husband's frequent absences? Is it because it frees up her own time to pursue her own secret life? Has her husband's timing caught her too on the rebound from an aborted liaison? Or is she just overwhelmed with relief that he knows nothing, when she fears he might know everything? These are questions the film prompts after its ending, even though Frédéric is too stupid and narcissistic to pose them to himself, and which it has made no attempt to answer, only to pose obliquely through the strategy of default. This is where Rohmer's modernism is just as original in its own way as that of his New Wave colleagues and where he departs, significantly, from Bergman's classicism of the 1950s, with which he still has much in common. Suffice to say, the parallel modernisms of Bergman and Rohmer are worlds apart. *Love in the Afternoon* is nothing like the Baltic trilogy that Bergman had made during the period of the later *Moral Tales*. But if it is not, it is because Bergman, not Rohmer, had changed direction so completely.

CHAPTER FOUR

Existential Stoicism
Bergman–Antonioni

When Bergman and Michelangelo Antonioni died within a day of each other in 2007, Europe lost two of its greatest filmmakers. Their careers had begun at the end of the Second World War, their reputations had flourished in the 1960s, and their films of that decade glossed the troubled relationship between intimacy and modernity at the core of middle-class life. Bergman kept it tight, shooting almost exclusively on Fårö or in the studio. Intimacy was largely confined to triangles and quartets, often linked by family, inherently claustrophobic even in open landscapes, and, as a rule, far away from the city. Antonioni, by contrast, was more expansive. Starting in Rome, *L'avventura* (1964) seems to roam the whole of Sicily and its adjoining islands. Set in Milan, *La Notte* (1961) tracks the separate encounters with strangers of its troubled married couple. In Rome's classical centre and its modernist EUR suburb, *L'eclisse* (1962) charts the brief aborted intimacy of two beautiful young lovers who start off as strangers and end up as strangers, eclipsed by the city in which they live. In *Red Desert* Antonioni tackled something that Bergman would never have done, the destructive encounter of technology and nature: a poetic ecology in advance of its time. Using his muse and lover Monica Vitti as a barometer of love's malaise in all four films, there is a similarity between her intimate encounters and Bergman's variations on the troubled marriage using Liv Ullmann and Max von Sydow. Yet the troubled intimacy in Antonioni's city films that intrigued Bergman most was the one where Vitti (whose acting he professed not to admire) was in a secondary role. It was the faltering marriage of Jeanne Moreau – whom he did admire – and Marcello Mastroianni in *La Notte* which intrigued him most, and we can see its impact a year later on *Winter Light*.

Near the end of his life, Bergman's ambivalent attitude to Antonioni, whom he sometimes admired and sometimes criticized, hardened. He liked the tense and tightly edited city films, *La Notte* and *Blow-Up* (1966); for the rest he claimed to care very little. Apart from these two features, Bergman found the Italian's editing too slack and loose, sacrificing montage to mise en scène, in search of the great shot and great scene at the expense of tension, drama and continuity (Aghed

2002:192). Here he likened Antonioni to Dreyer in one key respect. Both could produce great images but both were, technically speaking, 'amateurs' (Simon 1971:78). We might want to dismiss this judgment as part of the tetchiness of age. Bergman had no reason to feud with Antonioni, who had always been respectful of his work. But another way to look at this outburst would be to see 'amateurs' as a codeword for 'rivals'. Bergman shared with Dreyer a cinematic response to the crisis in Protestant faith; he shared with Antonioni an intense preoccupation with the malaise of modern intimacy. Bergman felt happier praising Fellini, Kurosawa and Tarkovsky because, one feels, they were more distant. While there were solid overlaps with all three, they did not directly encroach on his territory. The two 'amateurs' did. They both, we could speculate, hit a raw nerve.

Yet *L'avventura*, which Bergman berated for its longueurs, must have been a key reference point for him. Remoteness of setting, coastal landscapes, troubled figures in isolation: Bergman had equally used all these motifs in his first Fårö film – *Through a Glass Darkly* – released a year later. The geographic relation of the Lipari Islands to Sicily bears an uncanny resemblance to Fårö lying just off the north-west coast of Gotland: a Mediterranean mirror image of the Baltic. The different range of the two films is also key. Bergman's is a tight chamber drama *en famille*, while Antonioni's is a lingering expansive adventure film, which plays on encounters with strangers. The mystery of the missing girl, which is never resolved in *L'avventura*, is far from Bergman's dark, explicit psychodrama. But that same ambience of landscape and mystery resurfaces ten years later in the most enigmatic film of the Baltic trilogy: *A Passion*. It is open ended in the Antonioni sense: a mystery of event that is also a mystery of landscape. If Antonioni was more expansive, he was also more restless, wanting to make films around the world, while Bergman stuck firmly to his native country. The results favoured Bergman. His productivity remained high. Antonioni's career went into decline, often defeated by the logistics of his ambition. Yet out of that ambition, Antonioni left Italy and delivered three major films that embraced other countries and other cultures: his London mystery *Blow-Up*, his Chinese documentary *Chung Kuo* (1972), and the unique meeting of Europe and North Africa that is present in the puzzle of *The Passenger* (1975). Bergman left Sweden only because he felt he had to, as a tax exile, and then to the country he judged the culturally closest to his own – Germany.

Bergman's admiration of *La Notte* and *Blow-Up* centred on time compression. If Antonioni was more expansive in his use of film space, then Bergman only saw that working narratively when he imposed limits on duration. Both Antonioni's films last roughly twenty-four hours, starting and ending in early morning. Both unfold within city limits – Milan and London – and both end in open spaces: a golf course and a park. Both are fables for a consumer age of wasted wealth and wasted artistry. There is nothing as radical, socially speaking, in Bergman's films of the same decade. The trials and tribulations of the cultural capital are more peripheral to his work and the city is off limits for nearly all his features. Likewise, Bergman's films unfold against the background of a crisis in faith; Antonioni's films are secular in overt substance, despite the paradox that, personally, Antonioni remained a believer long after Bergman had abandoned his faith. Both directors are Nietzschean to a point, but *La Notte* also turns the hermetic discourse of Adorno on twentieth-century culture into an accessible world of signs.

For all this *La Notte* had a radical impact on Bergman's transformation of style – his new use of ellipsis, his taut refined minimalism, his pared down performances. Several points of contact stand out in *Winter Light*: the time limit with Bergman taking his film down to a three-hour duration from midday to three o'clock on a winter afternoon, the crucial role of the letter in the exposure of bruised intimacy, the consistent use of long shots and the selective heightening of ambient sound. For example, the scene in *La Notte* when Lidia leaves the party in the car with a complete stranger, the sound of their talk, shot from outside the car, is drowned out by torrential rain and screen wipers on full throttle. The *Winter Light* equivalent is the long shot by the river, where police remove the body of the suicide Jonas Persson and their conversation with Tomas is drowned out by the roaring rapids. The letter sequences are more central, and contrasting. Whereas Giovanni, the celebrity writer of *La Notte,* fails to recognize his previous letter to Lidia that she reads him in the film's final sequence, Bergman shifts his letter sequence back much earlier in the narrative and reverses gender. Giovanni blanks out the passion of his earlier writing, while Pastor Thomas fearfully postpones reading the long letter Märta has written him. When he eventually starts, Bergman cuts sharply from his words to those of Märta, shot in extreme close-up. She addresses the camera for over six minutes, as if her voice alone can propel the letter forward to its bitter conclusion and also, perhaps, as if hearing the words in her voice, not his, could be the only thing that gives the letter the necessary momentum to reach its bitter end. In both cases the woman reads the letter to reveal a moment of truth about which the listening man is evasive. Lidia uses the letter to remind Giovanni of a lost passion, and Märta's letter laments the failure of their passion to gain lift off after the death of Thomas's wife.

The stillborn relationship of Tomas and Märta is one in which Bergman effectively blends theatrical with cinematic heritage. The former is Nordic, the latter truly European. The story of a pastor living in rural isolation, who cannot shake off the ghost of his dead wife, is inherited from Ibsen's *Rosmersholm*, with Pastor Tomas as a contemporary update on the tight, tense John Rosmer and Märta as an unflamboyant, eczematous Rebecca West. The Ibsen tragedy was one that Bergman had planned to direct in Stockholm in the late 1960s with Liv Ullmann and Max von Sydow: plans that never came to fruition. But you could argue that he had already transplanted it to his cinema. Here dramatic tragedy as a stage form is superseded in *Winter Light* by something more cinematic – an existential stoicism that Bergman appropriated from Antonioni in changing the nature of his own cinema. The tragic repetition that marks Ibsen's chamber drama (where the mill-race claims the lives of the play's central trio) is replaced by the will to endure in *Winter Light*. The Antonioni precedent comes, not only in *La Notte*, but also in *L'avventura*, where the sudden disappearance of Anna, Sandro's fiancée, creates an absent presence which haunts the footsteps and feelings for each other of Sandro and her best friend Claudia. The faltering marriage of *La Notte* flavours present time. The absent presence in *L'avventura* informs time past and *Winter Light* brings them together – the haunting with the here and now.

In the 1960s, Antonioni and Bergman present us with a post-tragic cinema – one that goes beyond the centrality of tragic loss, without at the same time offering reconciliation or redemption; and one that is a clear alternative to the way in which popular cinema often reheats melodrama to pass itself off as tragedy. Bergman moves on from the portentous presence of Death that defines *The Seventh Seal* and conversely the healing of time that ends *Wild Strawberries*. Antonioni moves on from the suicidal melancholia that defines and at times suffocates *Il grido* (1957). This, it could be argued, is one of the central turning points of film modernism – an existential stoicism both directors share with early Resnais, later with Wim Wenders and at times with Bresson. While many of the great films of the New Wave – *Breathless*, *Jules and Jim*, *Pierrot le fou*; and of New American cinema – *Bonnie and Clyde* (1967), *Five Easy Pieces* (1970), *Nashville* (1975) and *Chinatown* (1974), explore new forms of tragicomedy and while Buñuel and Fellini reinvent comedy as an acerbic modernist form, Antonioni and Bergman share something that perhaps goes deeper in its challenge to our sensibilities. It is they who respond most directly to the death of tragedy in modern writing, through their focus on contemporary middle-class life, on devoted professionals and the veil of prosperity that surrounds them and often enervates them.

Stylistically, however, the differences are vast. Bergman worked through the northern expressionist tradition: a stage director who absorbed theatricality into his screen art. His world was still, however, obliquely demonic and the enigmas of the human face were firmly at the centre of his vision. Antonioni worked out of the southern documentary form of neo-realism, but drained it of dramatic force to make it more abstract and architectural. Resolutely secular, he was more concerned with the positioning of the subject against the cityscape or landscape, rather than with the mysteries of the human face. Yet there are points of convergence and we can see these clearly in the context of French culture in the 1930s and 1940s, as a connecting link above all in the films of Marcel Carné and the writings of Albert Camus, where the legacy of poetic realism combines with the imagistic reimagining of the existential text. That is to say, they take their French heritage in very different directions, but their visions have a common root. This is illustrated more clearly by comparing two films that have a different format, a different look, a very different style of acting and a totally different form of staging, that take this common legacy in very opposite and very original directions: *The Silence* and *The Passenger*.

The Silence and *The Passenger* are two of the greatest modernist films of their period, and two of the most enduring. From the standpoint of a new century, neither seem dated. Yet their genesis lies in a previous era to their own, that of French classical cinema and the rise of existentialism in philosophy and writing. The former produced one of the France's great film directors, Marcel Carné, and the latter one of its great modern writers Albert Camus. This is all the more remarkable since neither France nor French culture is conspicuously present in either picture. *The Silence* is an intimate chamber drama set in a fictitious Eastern European country and *The Passenger* takes place in two continents, Europe and Africa, and four named countries: Chad, England, Germany and Spain. While both are films about journeys to foreign countries, the methods of filming are utterly different. In essence Bergman delivered a tight interior shoot at the Råsunda studios, while Antonioni's film for MGM was a logistically complex location feature that added one extra (non-diegetic) country, Algeria, in its shoot for the desert sequences.

The French Connection

As Peter Cowie notes, *The Silence* is coloured by Bergman's memories of European cities, of Hamburg just after the war when the streets were still patrolled by tanks (Bergman also mentions in his memoir a brief teenage stop off in a dark, silent pre-war Berlin); and in France, memories of a summer hotel in Grenôble and a Paris hotel where he had a brief assignation, and whose view resembled the street seen from the window of the room used for sex by Anna and the waiter (Cowie 1992:211). We could add to these, perhaps, the attraction of the onscreen hotels designed for Marcel Carné by Alexander Trauner in the aptly named *Hôtel du Nord* (1938), and in *Port of Call* (1948), where Jean Gabin and Michèle Morgan spend the last hours of their doomed romance. Bergman thus blends the hotels of his own memories with the hotels in cinema of one of his favourite directors. Just as Gabin is a fugitive in Le Havre, 'travelling through' in *Le quai des brumes* (1938), so Bergman's family trio in *The Silence* are also travelling through; their foreign city a stopover rather than a destination. This is a film in which the encounter with strangeness is paramount and that too is a feature of Antonioni's *The Passenger*. Both films pose the question: in a strange world that is sudden and different, how do we read the signs? Whereas the intimate dramas of the hotel are the key link with Carné, the encounter with strangeness is the key link with Albert Camus and both directors responded strongly to Carné and Camus at roughly the same time: at the start of their film careers.

If there is a tilting towards Carné's romantic fatalism in Bergman's early films, like *It Rains on our Love* (1946) and *Port of Call* we could argue that *The Silence*, much more abstract, echoes the fatalism with little trace of the romance. Like *Le quai des brumes* the latter is also a brilliant dissection of jealousy *en famille* with a subtextual prehistory. Carné's jealous guardian, Michel Simon, is horrified by his young ward's attraction to Jean Gabin because, we guess, it exacerbates a forbidden desire for the teenage girl in his charge (and may echo transgressions already committed). Bergman achieves the same with Ingrid Thulin as Ester, a jealous older sister, humiliated by her sibling Anna's brute desire for a complete stranger. If we take the interior look of Bergman's picture, we can see that Carné's legacy, complete with baroque *mise en scène*, permeates its dreamlike hotel atmospherics (at which the Frenchman specialized) and its sense of an enclosed, designed world full of sharp, off-kilter detail. In both its look and its feel *The Silence* references *Hôtel du Nord* and *Le quai des brumes*. Yet there is a key contrast. If the Carné hotel is a familiar site, then Bergman's is most definitely a site of the uncanny.

If, on the other hand, there is a tilting towards Camus in *The Passenger*, it is because the existential crisis of its Anglo-American protagonist in North Africa echoes those in Camus's famous novel *L'Étranger (The Outsider)* (1937) and his desert stories of *L'Exil et le royaume (Exile and the Kingdom)* (1957). Yet we can easily switch things around. Antonioni started his film career as an assistant director for Carné during the war on *Les visiteurs du soir* (1944), and as a postwar critic in Italy was to acclaim several of Carné's films in a period when the Frenchman's reputation was already on the slide (Turk 1989:197, 297). Bergman, meanwhile, directed Camus's existential power drama *Caligula* early in his stage career and towards the end of the 1950s was in negotiation with the independent Hecht-Lancaster company and with Camus himself to direct an adaptation of *La Chute (The Fall)* for the big screen, a project aborted by the Frenchman's fatal car crash in 1960 (Björkman et al. 1973:26–27).

It is a fascinating crossover. After the Second World War, the young Bergman proclaimed Carné's poetic realism as the way forward for cinema, while as late as 1994 the veteran Bergman still included *Le quai des brumes* in his top eleven films of all time. Likewise, Bergman had also expressed his dislike of the films of Jean Renoir, Carné's close rival, who openly denounced *Le quai des brumes* as 'fascist' on its release in pre-war France (Andrew 1995:267–68). In his 1968 interviews with Swedish critics for *Bergman on Bergman*, the Swedish director also acknowledged the impact of existentialism on his work and claimed Camus's version of that nebulous philosophy to be more 'refined' than Sartre's (Björkman et al. 1973:12–13).

With Antonioni we can explore a different kind of configuration. If anything, his connection to Carné and Camus had been even more immediate. While waiting in Nice in wartime France for a visa to join Carné as an assistant director in Paris, the Italian stayed at the Negresco hotel where he become one of the first Italians to read the just-published *L'Étranger*. He read it in a single sitting, astonished by its power and vision. At the same time, Antonioni tells us, he was planning a film about a grand hôtel, prompted by the scale of the Negresco and by the boredom of his month-long stay waiting to enter occupied France (Antonioni 2007:250). He would also have been aware that Carné was himself a maestro of the hotel setting, though Carné's historical film – *Les visiteurs du soir* – on which he got a credit (and contributed nothing), was a historical oddity, far away from the world of hotels. Instead, it seems he was hooked on an idea of a 'Carné' hotel informed by Camus's flair for existential abstraction. So Antonioni worked for a week as a room-service waiter to get a sense of the functioning of the building, and started writing a screenplay, which he then lost (ibid.:250–51). Later, he resisted the temptation to film *L'Étranger*, which Visconti did only to make an insipid film. Instead, Antonioni absorbed the spirit and themes of Camus into his own work. Camus's writing and Carné's hotel scenario were finally to coalesce thirty years later in *The Passenger*. If Antonioni's experience of working under Carné proved totally discomforting, the one thing he took from it was the Frenchman's shrewd placement of the camera. And he was also gracious enough, as a postwar critic, to champion several of Carné's films, when the Frenchman's reputation was already in decline. One final observation came out of Antonioni's stay at the seafront Negresco in 1961, when he saw a drowned man float in with the tide onto the beach, and a little girl cry out at the terrible sight, before the police arrived to dispose of the corpse. Antonioni comments that if he made a film of this, he would film the setting without the event and focus instead on his state of mind as a witness, waiting endlessly in the middle of a war: '[T]he true emptiness, the malaise, the anxiety, the nausea, the atrophy of all normal feelings and desires, the fear, the anger – all these I felt when, coming out of the Negresco, I found myself in that whiteness, in that nothingness, which took shape around a black point' (ibid.:53). These were the observations of a film director who had read Camus, reflecting back in the language of Camus to the time when he had first read him and setting up the future sensibility that would become, in the penultimate sequence of *The Passenger*, a different kind of hotel exit altogether.

What Antonioni shares in common with Carné is the designed architectural look of his images. While Carné's studio films are usually an atmospheric studio abstraction from city locations – a Le Havre, for example, that is half real and half imagined – Antonioni is master of the location shoot that renders strange the actual physiognomy of a living city – Milan in *La Notte*, Rome in *L'eclisse*, and London in *Blow-Up*. While Antonioni fuses Carné with the architectural look of neo-realism, *The Silence*, on the other hand, crosses Carné with the *Kammerspiel* effect of the Scandinavian masters – Ibsen, Strindberg and Dreyer. Yet both modernist directors then go on to transcend their sources. They move away from the staged melodrama of classical film into a world of oblique signs, where plotlines are never clear and strangeness overpowers the familiar – a world that is existential and uncanny at the same time.

As the works of artists who began their careers during the war, it is important to see *The Silence* and *The Passenger* as films which simultaneously combine wartime and postwar experiences. *The Silence* is a film in which preparation for war rumbles on and recalls the anxieties of 1939, but it also has a Cold War edge, made as it was just after the construction of the Berlin Wall and just before the Cuban Missile Crisis. One feels that its imaginary city behind the Iron Curtain has this doubled historical identity. In the case of Antonioni, his wartime service with the Italian army in the North African desert makes *The Passenger* a film about returning in more ways than one. Here the war/postwar conundrum resonates equally as colonial/postcolonial, and the setting of *L'Étranger*, the novel that affected him so much in this film, becomes both violent and colonial in its perverse and distanced purity. The north–south European divide of both directors and their films suggests equidistance, too, from the world of Carné. Bergman typically reinvents poetic realism in his studio shoot by making it oblique, abstract and uncanny. Antonioni transforms it into the world of the multiple location shoot, traversing countries and continents. The injection of Camus into Carné's world is part and parcel of this double transformation. Just as *L'Étranger* is a book about strangeness, so *The Silence* and *The Passenger* render the familiar unfamiliar, through the pivotal role of the hotel as the place of transience. In black and white, Bergman reduces the modern city to a compressed non-identity; in colours at times intense, Antonioni deconstructs the enterprise of tourist exotica and reinvents the travelogue as nightmare. Hotels are the repositories of adventures in foreign lands where the differences in language and culture create a restricted vocabulary of signs.

The Camus Paradigm

The literary writing of Camus offers a bridge between the classical and the modern in the culture of the last century because, at its best, it explores the abiding centrality of strangeness in modernity, and does it on a terrain that is deceptively familiar. Camus specializes in de-familiarizing the natural object or the natural condition, rendering it strange with a calm and blinding lucidity. In *L'Étranger*, Mersault leads a humdrum life in Algiers, yet fails to grieve over his mother's death and commits murder for no clear reason, as an *acte gratuit*. There is a chilling edge to Mersault's banal existence ending in that murder, which has a universal resonance.

Both in his fiction and stage plays Camus's existential view of the human condition is not humanist – as many believe and he himself claimed – but thoroughly Nietzschean in its agonistic vision of the operation of power. It was Sartre who reassured us in his acclaimed postwar essay that existentialism was 'a humanism' (Sartre 1948). Yet Camus goes in the opposite direction. Plays like *Caligula, Le Malentendu (Cross Purpose)* and *Les Posédés (The Possessed)* take the spectator to the very abyss of nothingness, through a calculated strategy of probing the limits of nihilism. His fiction, meanwhile, cues us into its deadly obsessions through the titling strangeness of *L'Étranger*; the metaphorical (yet metonymic) and doomed kingdom of North African exile in *Exile and the Kingdom*; the sardonic, existential fallen-ness of *The Fall*. In all of these texts the dynamics of power are Nietzschean, menacing and ubiquitous.

Antonioni and Bergman focus on different spheres of the Camus paradigm. In *The Silence*, Bergman explores the power dynamics of troubled intimacy that affects sisters in a forbidding hotel in a foreign land. He moulds his narrative obliquely, as a Cold War fable. The existential strangeness of a hostile country on the brink of war is a measure for the outwardly assured but inwardly troubled Bergman of the time; of God's 'silence' in a world without transcendent values. If Bergman's film has a Cold War northern European feel to it, the Mark Peploe screenplay for Antonioni's *The Passenger* looks south in its take on the complex power relations in the new Africa of the 1970s. Thus the estranged colonial subject of Camus's North African fiction – firmly *pied noir* – has been replaced, a generation later, by the 'impartial' anglophone reporter on roughly the same terrain. While Camus' poor French colonials cling to landscapes that fascinate and alienate in equal measure, the postcolonial case is different. Antonioni's reporter Locke is upended by his logos of BBC neutrality, the new British quest for 'objectivity', that is meant to signify the absolute end of colonial power and a new enlightened positioning, but which is febrile to say the least. Yet Locke follows the pattern of Mersault's double exile, estranged from North Africa, and also from his homeland (in this case England not France). His deranged desert epiphany mirrors the trauma of Camus's evangelical missionary in *Le Renégat ou un esprit confus (The Renegade or a Confused Mind)* kidnapped by fetishists in a desert town of salt. But it also echoes the salesman's 'unfaithful' wife in *La Femme adultère*, who escapes at dead of night from their hotel in a remote fortress town, to experience orgasmic communion with the desert and the stars. A common thread runs through these contrasting situations. The oblique power games are intimately connected with a breakdown of language: equivalence of foreign land and foreign tongue is a form of dislocation in voice and image, often poetic, sometimes hypnotic. The first hotel sequence of *The Silence* and the first desert sequence in *The Passenger* make it clear that not only the voices are foreign, but also the culture's visual signs.

Hotel Passions: Carné and Bergman

Like Carné, Bergman's focus is on the hotel that is never seen from the outside. Its identity is exclusively interior: extensive in design, claustrophobic in feeling. In *The Passenger*, the hotel is inside and outside – a series of stopping places, small and grand – starting in the Chad desert and ending up at the 'Hotel de la Gloria' in Osuna. The Antonioni hotel is a multiple, an aggregation, a composite, a one-hotel-after-the-other, that starts and ends in perfect symmetry with a death that is never truly explained: the death of Robertson, the arms dealer, whose identity Locke the reporter then assumes, only to die at the end in almost identical circumstances. The difference between Antonioni and Bergman is that of movement and stillness. Bergman cuts elliptically from the sisters' train journey to the city hotel itself. They are, as it were, already magically embedded there. Antonioni's film is a constant journey from one place to another, of checking in and out of hotels, entering and leaving. Yet as we shall see, the interiors of the Chad and Osuna hotels, designed by Piero Poletto – both shot in Almeria, both with panelled doors – share both their look and their protagonist's fate. In this story of the double, the visual resemblance of Locke and Robertson (Jack Nicholson and Chuck Mulvehill) is mirrored in the doubling of the respective hotels where they meet their death. In *The Silence* everything that takes place outside the foreign hotels has issue inside it, and *The Passenger* sets this in the plural. The exterior event echoes in the internal setting.

These modernist departures are compelling because they retain Carné's trope of hotel destiny, while utterly transforming the sensibility. While the hotel room remains the key site of fate for Bergman, it is no longer the site of romantic doom. In Carné, we are transfixed in the hotel room that is the last haven of desperate lovers Jean (Jean Gabin) and Nelly (Michèle Morgan) before the fugitive Gabin perishes melodramatically; or by the daily dramas of the Hôtel du Nord, where Arletty is finally shot to death in her room. No contrast is greater between Bergman and Carné than this: the morning-after scene between Jean and Nelly in *Le quai des brumes*, their poignant leave taking before he boards ship for Venezuela and the steamy, oppressive pick-up sequence in *The Silence,* where in defiance of Ester, her dying sister, Anna (Gunnel Lindblom) brings a predatory waiter (Birger Malmsten) back to their hotel and beds him defiantly in the room opposite. In Carné's film, Gabin is the rock-like male subject, tough, fugitive, an army deserter on the run, whose fate we hypnotically follow. In Bergman's film, Malmsten, who had played ersatz Gabin roles in earlier films like *It Rains on our Love* and *Three Strange Loves*, now gives his best performance for Bergman a decade later as the foreign waiter, when he becomes the ghost of Gabin and transforms him into pure object, when he objectifies the icon as ineffable object of female lust without voice or language, and thus reduces him to blankness. In the realm of God's silence this bleak film inhabits, the echo of human perfidy is to be found in those tactical silences of calculated lust, which Malmsten calibrates to perfection. Bergman thus replaces Carné's doomed romanticism with a tight claustrophobic power play. The quartet of two warring sisters, tiny bemused son and his mother's silent lover, in facing hotel rooms, is in a veritable antechamber of hell – Bergman's *Huis Clos.* The mise en scène is so totally interior (and studio-bound) there is not one exterior shot of the hotel in which the two sisters and young boy are caged. In this drastic economy of scale any homage to Alexandre Trauner, Carné's great set designer of street exteriors, is conspicuous by its absence. We should also note the poetic harshness of Sven Nykvist's high-contrast photography, in complete contrast to the soft oneiric diffusions of light in Carné's Le Havre of mist and shadow. Bergman's monochrome extremity is pitiless and takes no prisoners.

Gabin and Nicholson: The Fugitive Kind

If *The Silence* is indebted to *Le quai des brumes* in its staging, atmospherics and hotel-room destiny, themewise, *The Passenger* owes Carné an even greater debt (though how conscious this is, we do not know). In Carné's film Gabin, the army deserter, plans to escape France by sailing to Venezuela and by taking another man's identity, through doctoring the passport of a painter (Robert Le Vigan) he met in the port and who subsequently drowns in a freak accident. Near the start of *The Passenger* Locke (Jack Nicholson), after his breakdown epiphany when searching for desert rebels he fails to find, decides to become a fugitive by doctoring the passport of a lookalike Englishman, Robertson (Chuck Mulvehill), who has died suddenly in their remote Chad hotel. He then abdicates his identity as reporter and assumes, as he later finds out, the dead man's identity as gunrunner with its ensuing risks. In both cases, we see an attraction of opposites in the transfer: fugitive soldier/modern artist, television reporter/arms dealer. In Carné's film the subterfuge briefly works to move on the plot; but in Antonioni's existential travelogue it slowly and agonizingly falls apart and becomes the subject of the film. Everyone – friends, police, secret agents, ex-wife and current lover – is after Locke in the famous final long take of the picture at the Hotel de la Gloria in Osuna. The slow forward then circular shot out of his barred hotel window, which quickens as it turns 180 degrees to film the window from the outside, shows Locke's past catching up with him, as the burnt-out reporter, who has sought freedom in subterfuge, is finally trapped by what he dearly wished to escape, the baggage and ballast of his former life. Released from the constricting, failed identity he has shed, he is kidnapped by its clear residues and killed by the fatal risks of the one he has taken in its place.

If Bergman's nameless waiter objectifies the figure of Gabin, Antonioni's reporter retains a Gabin-like subjectivity in Nicholson's brilliant performance, but the film also objectifies him by reinventing him, and at the same time dissecting the past profession he has abandoned with a clinical, documentary eye. This is mirrored precisely in the archive film clip watched by his estranged wife, Rachel, and closest friend, Ian Hendry. In it, Locke's African witch doctor suddenly turns the camera round on Locke himself in the middle of the reporter's interview. With the reinvented Locke the paradox becomes foundational: the narrative forges a persona who is truly existential, but only by being someone other, by creating for himself a virtual non-self. While Gabin's Jean is quick in a crisis to react, to raise his voice or use his fists, he is solidly knowable. Nicholson's reinvented Locke (now Robertson) is cool, affable, seemingly at peace with 'himself'. His crisis appears over.

Yet his change of identity is paradoxically a change of skin, a change to calmness and stoicism after his reporter's epiphany of rage in the desert, or the flashback book burning in the garden of his London home, that signifies his flair for self-destruction and the end of his marriage. Perhaps calmness is the last thing we would expect from someone facing the dangers of his adopted profession – trading in guns to African rebels. Yet danger gives him an inner peace where professional 'objectivity' has unhinged him and he comes face to face with the subjects that had previously eluded him. There is a fleeting likeness in the ending of the two pictures that should also be noted. The fugitive Jean seals his fate by returning impulsively from the portside ship bound for Venezuela to say goodbye to Nelly one last time. On his return, we see him shot in the street by his love rival, gangster Pierre Brasseur. Bound for the ferry that will take him to Morocco and thence perhaps, to his point of origin in the Chad desert, the fugitive Locke seals his fate by electing to go en route via the Hotel de la Gloria in Osuna, marked as the last meeting place in Robertson's diary. He keeps his alter ego's appointment when he has no need to, and dies. The shot that kills him (if indeed there is one) is heard offscreen, when he too is offscreen, in the middle of the penultimate take. It is a bold double absence. In *Le quai des brumes* we witness full-on melodramatic ending; in *The Passenger* the camera is pointing in the other direction.

How Uncanny is Freud's 'Uncanny'?

So much has been written about Freud's version of the uncanny, there seems little point in adding to it. But let us consider this. The key illustration his essay gives the reader from his own life is highly scenic, highly visual: it evokes a landscape we might associate with De Chirico or later with Antonioni. Walking one hot summer afternoon in the deserted streets of a southern Italian town, Freud had lost his sense of direction and returned (involuntarily?) three times to the same labyrinthine part of town where the streets were narrow and 'Nothing but women with painted faces were to be seen at the windows of the small houses'. 'I found myself in a quarter', he comments tortuously, 'of whose character I could not remain long in doubt' (Freud 1985:359). This uncanny repetition of the same not only conceals unspoken desire (amusing here where the joke is on Freud), but also evokes in his failure to escape the labyrinth, 'the sense of helplessness experienced in some dream states'. Eventually Freud, his presence now conspicuous in the quarter of disrepute, does escape, making his way back to the town piazza with great relief. But the point is made. In the off-kilter perspectives of De Chirico's paintings – their 'making strange' of classical design that Antonioni often injects into his cinematic staging of Italian townscapes – there is a sense of the familiar made unfamiliar; the classical, transparent and reassuring, now angular, threatening, asymmetrical. And it is dreamlike; it does convey helplessness, because it concerns the return of the same. It is, in a word, uncanny.

The uncanny is an ocular, architectural trope that resonates through Antonioni's Italian trilogy *L'avventura*, *La Notte* and *L'eclisse*. Here in *The Passenger* it is less central, except at key moments. One such moment is Locke's double sighting of the twice-seated Girl (Maria Schneider), who claims to be an architecture student, first near a brutalist 1970s apartment block in Bloomsbury, then in the grand Modernista interior of Gaudi's Palau Güell in Barcelona. Another uncanny moment, of course, is Locke and Robertson as lookalike anglophone professionals in the same remote hotel in Saharan Africa. But the main moment of the uncanny is the actual doubling of Locke's hotels: the rundown hotel full of flies in the Chad village, where the distraught reporter swaps identities with the deceased gunrunner (how in fact did he die?), with the Hotel de la Gloria in Osuna, where Locke meets his end, and thus repeats the fate of his double. Since these occur right at the start and finish of the picture, they create an unusual and unexpected circular effect. The film may lack the visceral circularity of *Vertigo* or *Lost Highway* (1997), but its circular effect creeps up on the spectator unawares, creating an uncannily delayed reaction.

Open and Closed Worlds

By shedding his unwanted skin, Locke hopes to embrace an open world where any destination, Dubrovnik or Barcelona, is as good as any other. But by getting under the skin of his new persona, he is drawn back inexorably to the world he has abandoned. If any film has nailed the puzzle of free will and determinism that afflicts us all at some point in our lives, then this is it.

Locke thus appears to inhabit the open terrain of Europe, crossing frontiers at will, only for his past to catch him up and box him into a corner. He is both a free spirit, imitating a bird in flight on the cable car above the harbour in Barcelona, and a captive spirit, caged like one of the birds we see in the market stalls on the Ramblas. At the same time, it is his choice – with the apparent surety of the girl at his side, perfidious romance indeed – to take a second chance on Africa. In other words, if he escapes Osuna then the open desert awaits, but then, because his cover is already blown, there is no escape, no real either/or, no sanctuary. The cage is invisible but it is still there.

Antonioni's Uncanny

One of the clues to circularity lies in a specific sign of Antonioni's 'uncanny', a crucial detail: the identical look and design of the door panelling in the two hotel interiors. Ingeniously, art director Piero Poletto makes the doors and corridors of the Chad and Osuna hotels facsimiles, even though their interior colours differ. Indeed the hotels mainly contrast. Like Bergman's hotel in *The Silence*, the Chad hotel has no real exterior look. By contrast, the Osuna hotel defines itself through a truly uncanny exterior. And here, like Trauner's unnerving pencil-thin apartment block for Carné in *Daybreak*, the Antononi/Poletto design gives us something both naturalistic and surreal at the same time. In Carné's classic, the fugitive Gabin is holed out in his top-floor apartment of Trauner's studio edifice. But Antonioni's white stucco façade is basically single storey with an attic room, and looks more like the frontage of a tiny Andalucian town house on a dusty piazza (which it probably was before the director commandeered it for his movie, since, in its favour, it was opposite the stadium of a disused bullring). It is in fact a strange, madeover hotel on a deserted piazza, not in Osuna, but in Almeria, the arid region further east, where Antonioni shot most. if not all, of his Andalusia sequences and many of his African sequences too. Indeed, the first question the spectator asks on seeing the compact exterior is, 'Where are all the rooms?' There only seem to be two bedrooms – the adjoining rooms in which Locke and the Girl are staying. Thus the hotel has a truncated look, too squat and small, just as Trauner's 'tenement' in *Daybreak* is too thin and tall. It is that minor deviation from the norm that plants a seed of doubt in our minds about the reality of what we see.

Love is Strange

Le quai des brumes is a story of true love – alas fleeting and tragic. *The Silence* and *The Passenger* pose instead the question of betrayal, the former openly, the latter obliquely. Betrayal is everywhere in the movies, but here there are powerful variations. And, it could be argued, they come from that other French source linking the two films: the fiction of Camus. The most striking instance of sexual betrayal Camus evokes, comes in *La Femme adultère* (*The Adulterous Wife*), which opens the collection of stories in *L'Exil et le royaume*. Like *The Passenger*, it is both a desert story – a cold December bus journey by a French-Algerian couple to an oasis village on the southern high plateau; but also a hotel story, since the village hotel where they stay is the pivotal space around which the action revolves. The key, however, lies in the nature of the wife's 'adultery' that informs the story's title. Infidelity is not congress with another person, but with a place and a landscape of the Algerian interior, which at first sight is bleak and forbidding, but is then transformed for Janine, the middle-aged wife, into an unlikely site of desire. True, in *The Outsider*, Mersault has felt that in making love to his girlfriend he is also making love to the earth beneath her. And earlier, Janine has been fascinated by an encampment of distant nomads. But nothing prepares us for this. It is an extraordinary leap. As Brian Fitch comments, 'What more solipsistic enterprise could be devised than that of *an act of adultery committed in the absence of any other person but oneself?*' (Fitch 1988:122, original emphasis).

In one of the few stories Camus has framed through the eyes of a woman, there are multiplying forms of strangeness that Janine experiences: the bitter wind and winter cold of the desert on the bus ride, the self-contained world of Arabs in the interior shrouded in their burnouses, and the disagreeable pork and wine of their meal in the French-owned hotel that is an uncanny oasis within an oasis – an outpost of French cooking in a rural Muslim culture. *The Silence* also fuses foreignness and betrayal. Johannes, the boy, cannot understand the hotel desk clerk. The performing dwarfs that Anna watches in the cabaret, where she sees the copulating lovers, also stay at the hotel but do not speak Swedish either. They dress up the alarmed Johannes in girl's clothes, in a ritual with paedophile overtones. In both story and film, infidelity arises out of the trauma of the foreign. Pantheistically, Janine embraces the desert and the sky; Anna more materially, the foreign male body.

In Camus's story a double estrangement operates – the couple estranged from the culture and landscape of the interior, but also from each other. By the middle of the night when Janine escapes the hotel, husband and wife are barely on speaking terms, barely communicating. Theirs is a dying relationship the journey has finally made defunct. In *The Silence*, Bergman tunes up that estrangement-unto-death through a minimalist but powerful language of visual gesture. Prior to Anna's 'escape' from the hotel, the two sisters are barely communicating. Through an elaborate set of close shots and mirror shots, Bergman begins to generate a turning axis from rather than towards – a nexus of deflected bodies and deflected gazes. In one sequence this is mediated by the hapless Johannes, who physically bisects the distance between them, looking in vain to one and then the other for some shred of meaning in his disconcerting life.

Where Janine commits adultery within a foreign landscape, Bergman's treatment of betrayal is less metaphysical but more ambiguous. He allows us to see Anna's open betrayal of Ester with the voiceless waiter, but then poses the question 'betrayal of what?' Are, or were, the sisters incestuous? Or is one just cloyingly possessive of the other? And if so, what constitutes possession? Or do they just have to hate and humiliate in order to love each other all the more? This is what Kieślowski suggests is at the core of Bergman's film – the passage from hatred and humiliation into love (Kieślowski 2000:423). The vexed intimacy of the two sisters has at its end a kind of strange redemption. But does it? By dying, the older sister is left behind in the city.

Antonioni's film seems just the opposite to all this – the intimacy of complete strangers not estranged siblings, and it seems blithely to ignore the question of betrayal altogether. Maria Schneider is just a beautiful young woman passing through, who happens to be in the right or wrong place at the right or wrong time. This is adventure romance flattened out into a languorous road movie, where she takes everything as it comes – the open impulse of an impressionable girl hooked up with a man on the run. This is the story in the title, of the existential passenger who just goes along for the ride. Or is it? The Girl's timing of entrances and exits really does seem to be too impeccable. Like Eva Marie Saint in Hitchcock's *North by Northwest* (1959) she helps a fugitive to escape, but Hitchcock's heroine had another agenda as a CIA double agent, which soon becomes apparent. And after all, she is the one who delivers Cary Grant to the notorious prairie stop in the middle of nowhere, with its buzzing crop-duster that is inches away from taking his life. And it is the Girl who persuades Locke to keep his last appointment. But who exactly is she?

We never get to know; she never has any agenda that becomes apparent. Instead, she seems to epitomize Antonioni's zero-degree ideal of film character (which the treatment of Locke, of course, absolutely contradicts), where figures are what they do onscreen, with no past to constrain them. Yet eventually she helps deliver her lover to his death, seemingly by chance. We have to ask then, is that really so? There are no clear signs of duplicity and the film creates an intimacy between Locke and the Girl that is marked by its gentle humour and sensuous aura of calm, almost asexual at times in its delicacy and tenderness. There is none of the anguish or neurosis the director had evoked in his work with Monica Vitti. Word has it that Maria Schneider did not want to do any explicit sex scenes after the notoriety surrounding *Last Tango in Paris* (1972), and perhaps this was a blessing in disguise since in his later films Antonioni does not do sex scenes well. The single instance of the couple naked in their hotel room is a distant long shot through the bedroom window. It is precise, discreet and justified. At the same time it appears that close in-room shots of the naked couple making love were filmed and then cut from the final version (Chatman 2004:140–41). In retrospect the decision seems right. For this is a flight romance with long poignant moments of tranquillity, a strange, enduring love. But ... but ...

The Girl does seem to betray him. This is one reading that never leaves the viewer once the seed of suspicion is planted, and yet tantalizingly, this reading is never clinched by the penultimate shot. The field of interpretation remains open. In the film's poetics of repetition the seven-minute shot echoes the offscreen dynamics of the early desert sequences, where Locke, disoriented by the heat, the colours and intense light, comes up against the limits of his vision. The desert out-of-frame movement of distant figures into visual range, and off out again, confuses him. Antonioni's decentred editing supplements the effect. It is a trope the director repeats in his final sequence shot, where the enclosed, dusty piazza becomes a facsimile of the open desert. As one figure/object exits the frame, there is a brief void before the next figure/object enters.

When the view is from the window, Antonioni's moving shot makes virtuoso use of the out-of-frame image and noises off. Here too, there is a repeat of a previous *mise en scène*: the visual disorienting in the Chad desert. Antonioni's shot places the viewer one step behind the action while freeing up the motion of the camera to hover and fly like an out-of-body spirit, a transmigrating soul. Yet, like the reporter in the desert, the camera also misses out – it is ever so slightly off the pace. The brief time-lapse is telling, and in the end fatal. We cannot report on what we have not truly heard or seen. We can only speculate. In *The Silence* the camera is dark and forbidding and yet in the end we see everything; in *The Passenger* it is bright and translucent and yet we see nothing.

Figure 1 *'Summer Interlude* ... remains Bergman's purest and most romantic archipelago film' (p. 15).
Summer Interlude (Sommarlek) © 1951 AB Svensk Filmindustri. Stills Photographer: Louis Huch.
Bergman Archive 2.013

Figure 2 'One of the abiding images is that of starving platform hordes begging food from
passengers at train windows as the express pulls into a German station' (p. 19).
Three Strange Loves (Törst) © 1949 AB Svensk Filmindustri. Stills Photographer: Louis Huch.
Bergman Archive 1.097

Figure 3 'In Dreyer the uplifted face of suffering faces mortality but intimates the Beyond' (p. 33). *The Passion of Joan of Arc* (1928), Carl Theodor Dreyer. (The Joel Finler Archive)

Figure 4 'The Borgen farmhouse is not only the site of the sacred but also of the uncanny, homeliness made strange through its absorption of the universal' (p. 45). *Ordet* (1955), Carl Theodor Dreyer. (The Joel Finler Archive)

Figure 5 'The communion ceremony is formal and distant, the church freezing in early winter, all human warmth gone as ice grips the soul' (p. 45).
Winter Light (Nattvardsgästerna) © 1963 AB Svensk Filmindustri. Bergman Archive 4.028

Figure 6 '*Persona* uses the twentieth-century discourse of psychiatric healing to naturalize the vampire trope' (p. 40).
Persona (Persona) © 1966 AB Svensk Filmindustri. Bergman Archive 5.028

Figure 7 '...the coexistence of love and hate in heterosexual intimacy...' (p. 66).
Summer with Monika (Sommaren med Monika) © 1953 AB Svensk Filmindustri. Stills Photographer:
Louis Huch. Bergman Archive 2.029

Figure 8 Godard 'called his feuding lovers "the last romantic couple"...' (p. 65).
Pierrot le fou (1965), Jean-Luc Godard. (The Joel Finler Archive)

Figure 9 '... the hotel in which the two sisters and young boy are caged...' (p. 102).
The Silence (Tystnaden) © 1963 AB Svensk Filmindustri. Stills Photographer: Harry Kampf. Bergman Archive 4.069

Figure 10 'The slow forward then circular shot out of his barred hotel window ... shows Locke's past catching up with him...' (p. 103).
The Passenger (1975), Michelangelo Antonioni. (Reproduced with the kind permission of Jack Nicholson)

Figure 11 'It was the faltering marriage of Jeanne Moreau ... and Marcello Mastroianni in *La Notte* which intrigued (Bergman) most...' (p. 91).
La Notte (1975), Michelangelo Antonioni. (The Joel Finler Archive)

Afterword and Acknowledgements

John Orr died suddenly in 2010 while working on this book. He had been interested in writing on Bergman for some years, but as a writer on film he would only embark on a study of a major director if he felt that he had something new and fresh to add to the existing literature.

Viewing Bergman through the prism of modernity in a detailed comparison with other European directors gave John the original approach he desired, and the book as it now stands provides an intellectually rigorous discussion of Bergman and his place in twentieth-century film-making and the political, religious and philosophical currents of the period.

John Orr's original plan for this book had been that it would continue with a discussion of Fritz Lang and Michael Haneke called *The Austrian Connection*, exploring the influence of Lang, Brechtian narrative and violent killing especially in *From the Lives of the Marionettes*, and connections between Bergman and Haneke's use of the poetics of terror, ritual and offscreen violence. Then a chapter on Bergman and von Trier entitled *Oedipal*, was to elucidate von Trier's revolt against the strength of Bergman's legacy. With a chapter *The Power of Music* John planned to compare Wajda's melding of music and generational conflict in *Orchestra Conductor* with Bergman's in *Autumn Sonata* and *Saraband*. A final chapter, *Family Viewing*, would bring together Bergman with Terence Davies and Nuri Bilge Ceylan, of whom John Orr remarked: '*[B]oth Ceylan and Davies make great use of the still shot and both focus on the power (often tyrannical) of family*'.

Although these planned chapters would have carried Bergman's influence decisively into the twenty-first century, the existing chapters of this book do provide a sufficiently challenging reappraisal of Bergman's legacy to stand alone as a worthwhile monograph.

I would like to thank Peter Cowie and Maaret Koskinen for reading the manuscript and giving positive encouragement to go ahead with publication, and further thank Maaret for kindly agreeing to write a foreword. Special thanks to Martine Beugnet for the initial edit and in particular for her skilled compilation of the fourth chapter – combining this unfinished chapter and a previous article of John Orr's on Antonioni and Camus into a coherent whole.

Personal thanks to our daughter Katy for her careful editing of the text.

Anne Orr

Filmography

(Note: The English language title of Bergman's films is that used in the text, followed by Swedish title, and alternative U.K./U.S. titles. For directors other than Bergman, films are listed as they appear in the text plus foreign language title if commonly used.)

A Day in the Life of Andrei Arsenevitch. 1999. Chris Marker.
A Good Marriage, (Le beau marriage). 1982. Eric Rohmer.
A Lesson in Love, (En lection i kärlek). 1954. Ingmar Bergman.
A Letter to Three Wives. 1949. Joseph L. Mankiewicz.
A Married Woman, (Une femme mariée). 1964. Jean-Luc Godard.
A Passion, (En passion), (U.S. The Passion of Anna) 1969. Ingmar Bergman.
A Summer Tale, (Conte d'été). 1996. Eric Rohmer.
Ådalen 31. 1969. Bo Widerberg.
Alexander Nevsky. 1938. Sergei Eisenstein.
All These Women, (För att inte tala om alla dessa kvinnor), (U.K. Now about these Women). 1964. Ingmar Bergman.
Andrei Rublev. 1966. Andrei Tarkovsky.
Antichrist. 2009. Lars von Trier.
Autumn Sonata, (Höstsonaten). 1978. Ingmar Bergman.
Belle de jour. 1967. Luis Buñuel.
Blackmail. 1929. Alfred Hitchcock.
Blow-Up. 1966. Michelangelo Antonioni.
Bonjour Tristesse. 1958. Otto Preminger.
Bonnie and Clyde. 1967. Arthur Penn.
Breathless, (À bout de souffle). 1960. Jean-Luc Godard.
Brink of Life, (Nära livet), (U.K. So Close to Life). 1958. Ingmar Bergman.
Celine and Julie go Boating, (Céline et Julie vont en bateau). 1974. Jacques Rivette.
Chinatown. 1974. Roman Polanski.
Chung Kuo, Cina. 1972. Michelangelo Antonioni.
Citizen Kane. 1941. Orson Welles.
Claire's Knee, (Le genou de Claire). 1970. Eric Rohmer.
Close Encounters of the Third Kind. 1970. Steven Spielberg.
Cries and Whispers, (Viskningar och rop). 1972. Ingmar Bergman.
Day of Wrath, (Vredens Dag). 1943. Carl Theodor Dreyer.
Daybreak, (Le jour se lève). 1939. Marcel Carné.
Diary of a Country Priest, (Journal d'un curé de compagne). 1951. Robert Bresson.
Dreams, (Kvinnodröm), (U.K. Journey into Autumn). 1955. Ingmar Bergman.
8½, (Otto e mezzo). 1963. Federico Fellini.

Eternity and a Day, (Μια αιωνιότητα και μια μέρα, *Mia aioniotita kai mia mera*). 1998. Theo Angelopoulos.

Extase, (*Ecstasy*). 1933. Gustave Machatý.

Face to Face, (*Ansitke mot ansikte*). 1976. Ingmar Bergman.

Fanny and Alexander, (*Fanny och Alexander*). 1982. Ingmar Bergman.

Five Easy Pieces. 1970. Bob Rafelson.

From the Life of the Marionettes, (*Ur marionetternas liv*). 1980. Ingmar Bergman.

Full Moon in Paris, (*Les nuits de la pleine lune*).1984. Eric Rohmer.

Gang of Four, (*La Bande des quatre*). 1988. Jacques Rivette.

Hôtel du Nord. 1938. Marcel Carné.

Hour of the Wolf, (*Vargtimmen*). 1967. Ingmar Bergman.

Il grido, (*The Outcry*). 1957. Michelangelo Antonioni.

It Rains on our Love, (*Det regnar på vår kärlek*), (U.S. *The Man with an Umbrella*). 1946. Ingmar Bergman.

Ivan the Terrible, three parts. 1944–1946. Sergei Eisenstein.

J'entends plus la guitare, (*I can no longer hear the guitar*). 1991. Philippe Garrel.

Jules and Jim, (*Jules et Jim*). 1962. François Truffaut.

L'Âge d'or, (*The Golden Age*). 1930. Luis Buñuel.

L'amour fou, (*Mad Love*). 1969. Jacques Rivette.

L'avventura, (*The Adventure*). 1964. Michelangelo Antonioni.

L'eclisse, (*The Eclipse*). 1962. Michelangelo Antonioni.

La Notte, (*The Night*). 1961. Michelangelo Antonioni.

La Strada, (*The Road*). 1954. Federico Fellini.

Last Tango in Paris, (*Ultimo Tango a Parigi*). 1972. Bernardo Bertolucci.

Le Grand escroc, (*The Great Rogue*). 1963. Jean-Luc Godard.

Le Mépris, (*Contempt*). 1963. Jean-Luc Godard.

Le quai des brumes, (*Port of Shadows*). 1938. Marcel Carné.

Les Biches, (*Bad Girls*). 1968. Claude Chabrol.

Les visiteurs du soir, (*The Night Visitors*). 1944. Marcel Carné.

Lost Highway. 1997. David Lynch.

Love in the Afternoon, (*L'Amour d'àpres-midi*). 1972. Eric Rohmer.

Lust for Life. 1956. Vincente Minnelli.

M, (*Eine Stadt sucht einen Mörder*). 1931. Fritz Lang.

Masculine-Feminine, (*Masculin-féminin*). 1966. Jean-Luc Godard.

Mirror, (*Zerkalo*). 1975. Andrei Tarkovsky.

Mississippi Mermaid, (*La sirène du Mississipi*). 1969. François Truffaut.

Muriel, (*Muriel, ou le temps d'un retour*). 1963. Alain Resnais.

Nashville. 1975. Robert Altman.

Night and Fog, (*Nuit et brouillard*). 1955. Alain Resnais.

North by Northwest. 1959. Alfred Hitchcock.

Odd Man Out. 1947. Carol Reed.

Ordet, (*The Word*). 1955. Carl Theodor Dreyer.

Paris Belongs to Us, (Paris nous appartient). 1961. Jacques Rivette.

Paris vu par, (Six in Paris). 1965. Jean-Luc Godard et al.

Pauline at the Beach, (Pauline à la plage,. 1983. Eric Rohmer.

Persona. 1966. Ingmar Bergman.

Pierrot le fou. 1965. Jean-Luc Godard.

Port of Call, (Hamnstad). 1948. Ingmar Bergman.

Prison, (Fängelse), (U.S. The Devil's Wanton). 1949. Ingmar Bergman.

Raven's End, (Kvarteret Korpen). 1963. Bo Widerberg.

Red Desert, (Il Deserto Rosso). 1964. Michelangelo Antonioni.

Saraband. 2003. Ingmar Bergman.

Sauvage innocence, (Wild Innocence). 2001. Philippe Garrel.

Sawdust and Tinsel, (Gycklarnas afton). (U.S. The Naked Night). 1953. Ingmar Bergman.

Scenes from a Marriage, (Scener ur ett äktenskap). 1973. Ingmar Bergman.

Shame, (Skammen), (U.K. The Shame). 1968. Ingmar Bergman.

Smiles of a Summer Night, (Sommarnattens leende). 1955. Ingmar Bergman.

Soft Skin, (La peau douce). 1964. François Truffaut.

Solaris. 1972. Andrei Tarkovsky.

Stalker, (Сталкер). 1979. Andrei Tarkovsky.

Summer Interlude, (Sommarlek), (U.S. Illicit Interlude). 1951, Ingmar Bergman

Summer with Monika, (Sommaren med Monika), (U.S. Monika: The Story of a Bad Girl). 1953. Ingmar Bergman.

Sunset Boulevard. 1950. Billy Wilder.

The Blood of a Poet, (Le sang d'un poète). 1930. Jean Cocteau.

The Collector, (La collectionneuse). 1967. Eric Rohmer.

The Devil's Eye, (Djävulens öga). 1960. Ingmar Bergman.

The Face, (Ansiktet), (U.S. The Magician). 1958. Ingmar Bergman.

The Four Hundred Blows, (Les quatre cents coups). 1959. François Truffaut.

The Green Ray, (Le rayon vert). 1986. Eric Rohmer.

The Magic Flute, (Trollflöjten). 1975. Ingmar Bergman.

The Passenger, (Professione: reporter). 1975. Michelangelo Antonioni.

The Passion of Joan of Arc, (La passion de Jeanne d'Arc). 1928. Carl Theodor Dreyer.

The Passionate Friends. 1948. David Lean.

The Rite, (Riten), (also known as The Ritual). 1969. Ingmar Bergman.

The Sacrifice, (Offret). 1986. Andrei Tarkovsky.

The Serpent's Egg, (Ormens ägg). 1977. Ingmar Bergman.

The Seventh Seal, (Det sjunde inseglet). 1957. Ingmar Bergman.

The Sign of Leo, (Le signe du lion). 1959. Eric Rohmer.

The Silence, (Tystnaden). 1963. Ingmar Bergman.

The Story of Adèle H., (L'histoire d'Adèle H.). 1975. François Truffaut.

The Stranger, (Lo straniero). 1967. Luchino Visconti.

The Third Man. 1949. Carol Reed.

The Touch, (Beröringen). 1971. Ingmar Bergman.

The Umbrellas of Cherbourg, (*Les parapluies de Cherbourg*). 1964. Jacques Demy.

The Virgin Spring, (*Jungfrukällen*). 1960. Ingmar Bergman.

The Woman Next Door, (*La Femme d'à côté*). 1981. François Truffaut.

The Wrong Man. 1956. Alfred Hitchcock.

They Made Me a Fugitive. 1947. Alberto Cavalcanti.

Three Strange Loves, (*Törst*), (U.K. *Thirst*). 1949. Ingmar Bergman.

Through a Glass Darkly, (*Säsom i en spegel*). 1961. Ingmar Bergman.

To Joy, (*Till glädje*). 1950. Ingmar Bergman.

To Live my Life, (*Vivre sa vie*). 1962. Jean-Luc Godard.

Torment, (*Hets*). 1944. Alf Sjöberg.

Ulysses Gaze. 1995. Theo Angelopoulos.

Un Chien Andalou, (*An Andalusian Dog*). 1928. Luis Buñuel.

Vampyr, (*Der Traum des Allan Grey*). 1932. Carl Theodor Dreyer.

Vertigo. 1958. Alfred Hitchcock.

Voyage to Italy, (*Viaggio in Italia*). 1953. Roberto Rossellini.

Waiting Women, (*Kvinnors väntan*),(U.S. *Secrets of Women*). 1952. Ingmar Bergman.

Weekend, (*Le Weekend*). 1967. Jean-Luc Godard.

Wild Strawberries, (*Smultronstället*). 1957. Ingmar Bergman.

Winter Light, (*Nattvardsgästerna*), (U.S. *The Communicants*). 1963. Ingmar Bergman.

Selected Bibliography

Aghed, J. (2007 [2002]). 'Encounter with Ingmar Bergman', in R. Shargel (ed.). *Ingmar Bergman Interviews*. Jackson: The University Press of Mississippi, 190–200. (Originally published *Positif*, no. 497 July–August 2002).

Andrew, D. (1995). *Mists of Regret: Culture and Sensibility in Classic French Film*. Princeton: Princeton University Press, 1995.

Antonioni, M. (1963). *Michelangelo Antonioni: An Introduction*. Trans. S. Sullivan. New York: Simon and Shuster.

Antonioni, M. (2007). *The Architecture of Vision: Writings and Interviews on Cinema*, di C. Carlo, and G. Tinazzi (eds). American edition: M. Cottino-Jones (ed.). Chicago: The University of Chicago Press.

Aumont, J. (1997). *The Image*. Trans. C. Pajackowska. London: British Film Institute, BFI Publishing.

Aumont, J. (2003). 'Ingmar Bergman: "Mes films sont l'explication de mes images".' Paris: *Cahiers du cinéma/Éditions de l'Étoile*, 109–14.

Baldwin, J. (2007[1960]). 'The Northern Protestant', in R. Shargel (ed.). *Ingmar Bergman Interviews*. Jackson: The University Press of Mississippi, 10–20. (Originally published in *Esquire* (1960).)

Ballard, T. et al. (2010). 'Short Take Tributes on Rohmer.' *Senses of Cinema*, April 2010.

Bergala, A. (1980). 'De la vie des marionetces.' *Cahiers du cinéma*, 318/45, 1980.

Bergman, I. (1988). *The Magic Lantern: An Autobiography*. Trans. J. Tate. London: Penguin.

Bergman, I. (1995). *Images: My Life in Film*. Trans. M. Ruuth. London: Faber and Faber.

Bird, R. (2004). *Andrei Rublev*. London: British Film Institute, BFI Publishing.

Björkman et al. (1973). *Bergman on Bergman*. Trans. P.B. Austin. London: Martin Secker and Warburg.

Bonitzer, P. (1999). 'Eric Rohmer.' Paris: *Cahiers du cinéma/auteurs*.

Bordwell, D. (1981). *The Films of Carl-Theodor Dreyer*. Berkeley and Los Angeles CA: University of California Press.

Brody, R. (2008). *Everything is Cinema: The Working Life of Jean-Luc Godard*. London: Faber and Faber Ltd and New York: Metropolitan Books.

Chatman, S. and P. Duncan (eds). (2004). *Michelangelo Antonioni: The Investigation*. Köln: Taschen.

Comolli, J.-L. (1986 [1968]). 'Postscript: *Hour of the Wolf*', in J. Hillier (ed.). *Cahiers du cinéma Volume 2:1960-1968: New Wave, New Cinema, Re-evaluating Hollywood*. London: Routledge, 313–18. (Originally *Postface, Cahiers du cinéma* 203, August 1968.)

Comolli, J.-L. et al. (1965) 'Let's talk about *Pierrot*: An Interview with Jean-Luc Godard' *Cahiers du cinéma*, October 1965.

Cousins, M. (2004). *The Story of Film*. London: Pavilion.

Cowie, P. (1992). *Ingmar Bergman: A Critical Biography.* London: André Deutsch. (First published in 1982 by Martin Secker and Warburg.)

Dalle Vacche, A. (1996). *Cinema and Painting: How Art is Used in Film.* London: The Athlone Press.

Dixon, W.W. (2000). 'Persona and the 1960's Art Cinema', in L. Michaels (ed.). *Ingmar Bergman's Persona.* Cambridge: Cambridge University Press, 44–61.

Dreyer, C.T. (1973). *Dreyer in Double Reflection.* D. Skoller (ed. and trans. *Om Filmen* [*About the Film*]). New York: E.P. Dutton and Co, Inc.

Elsaesser, T. (2008). 'Ingmar Bergman's The Serpent's Egg: Reflections of Reflections on Retro-Fashion', in M. Koskinen (ed.). *Ingmar Bergman Revisited.* London and New York: Wallflower Press, 161–79.

Fitch, B. (1988). ' La Femme adultère: A Microcosm of Camus' solipsistic Universe', in A. Rizzuto (ed.). *Albert Camus' L'Exil et la royaume: The Third Decade.* Trinity College, Toronto: Les Editions Paratexte, 117–26.

Freud, S. (1985). 'The "Uncanny" (1919)', in *The Pelican Freud* Volume 14: Art and Literature. Harmondsworth: Penguin, 339–76.

Gillain, A. (1991). *François Truffaut: le secret perdu.* Paris: Hatier. (*Francois Truffaut: The Lost Secret*, trans. A. Fox. 2013 Indiana University Press.)

Godard, J.-L. (1958.) '*Bergmanorama.*' *Cahiers du cinéma* 85, July, 1958. Reprinted in T. Milne (ed.).

Godard, J.-L. (1986 [1967]). 'Struggling on Two Fronts: Godard in Interview', in J. Hillier (ed.) *Cahiers du cinéma Volume 2:1960–1968: New Wave, New Cinema, Re-evaluating Hollywood.* London: Routledge, 294–8. (Originally *Lutter sur deux fronts: conversation avec Jean-Luc Godard, Cahiers du cinéma* 194, October 1967.)

Hedling, E. (2008). 'The Welfare State Depicted: Post-Utopian Landscapes in Ingmar Bergman's Films', in M. Koskinen (ed.). *Ingmar Bergman Revisited.* London and New York: Wallflower Press, 180–93.

Johnson, V. and G. Petrie. (1994). *The Films of Andrei Tarkovsky: A Visual Fugue.* Bloomington and Indianapolis: Indiana University Press.

Kieślowski, K. (2000). 'Bergman's Silence.' Trans. P. Coates in J. Orr and O. Taxidou (eds). *Post-War Cinema and Modernity: A Film Reader,* Edinburgh: Edinburgh University Press, 422–5.

Koskinen, M. (2002). *I begynnelsen var ordet: Ingmar Bergman och hans tidiga författarskap.* Värnamo: Wahlström and Widstrand.

Koskinen, M. (2010). *Ingmar Bergman's The Silence.* Seattle: University of Washington Press.

Lasica, T. (1993). 'Tarkovsky's Choice.' *Sight & Sound,* March 1993 Vol. 3 Issue 3. London: BFI.

Livingston, P. (2008). 'On Ingmar Bergman and Philosophy: The Kaila Connection', in M. Koskinen (ed.). *Ingmar Bergman Revisited.* London and New York: Wallflower Press, 120–39.

Milne, T. (ed.). (1986). *Godard on Godard: Critical Writing by Jean-Luc Godard*. New York: Da Capo Press Inc.

Orr, J. (2008). 'Bergman, Nietzsche and Hollywood', in M. Koskinen (ed.). *Ingmar Bergman Revisited*. London and New York: Wallflower Press, 143–60.

Orr, J. (2010). *Romantics and Modernists in British Cinema*. Edinburgh: Edinburgh University Press.

Rivette, J. (1958). 'L'Âme au ventre.' *Cahiers du cinéma*, 84, June 1958, 45–7.

Rohmer, E. (1989). *The Taste for Beauty*. J. Narboni (ed.), trans. C. Volk. Cambridge: Cambridge University Press.

Ropars-Wuilleumier, M.-C. (2000 [1966]). ' Pierrot le fou', in D. Wills (ed.). *Jean-Luc Godard's* Pierrot le fou. Cambridge: Cambridge University Press, 178–81. (Originally published in *Esprit*, 34 [1966]).

Rosenbaum, J. (1995). *Placing Movies: The Practice of Film Criticism*. Berkeley and Los Angeles: University of California Press.

Rudkin, D. (2005) *Vampyr*. London: British Film Institute, BFI Publishing.

Sartre, J.P. (1948). *Existentialism and Humanism*. London: Methuen. (Originally (1946) *L'existentialisme est un humanisme*. Paris: Nagel.)

Simon, J. (2007 [1971]). 'Conversation with Bergman', in R. Shargel (ed.). *Ingmar Bergman Interviews*. Jackson: The University Press of Mississippi, 69–95.

Sjöman, V. (2007 [1963]). 'Excerpts from L136: Diary with Ingmar Bergman', in R. Shargel (ed.) *Ingmar Bergman Interviews*. Jackson: The University Press of Mississippi, 21–34.

Synessios, N. (2001). *Mirror*. London/New York: I.B. Tauris and Co. Ltd.

Tarkovsky, A. (1991). *Time Within Time: The Diaries 1970–1986*. Trans. K. Hunter-Blair. Calcutta: Seagull Books.

Tarkovsky, A. (2008). *Sculpting in Time: Reflections on the Cinema*. Trans. K. Hunter-Blair. Austin: University of Texas Press (11th printing).

Truffaut, F. (1980). *The Films of My Life*. Trans. L. Mayhew. London: Allen Lane, Penguin Books Ltd.

Turk, E. B. (1989). *Child of Paradise: Marcel Carné and the Golden Age of French Cinema*. Cambridge MA: Harvard University Press.

Index